WHAT ARE THEY SAYING ABOUT
THE LETTER OF JAMES?

What Are They Saying About
the Letter of James?

ALICIA J. BATTEN

Paulist Press
New York/Mahwah, NJ

Cover design by James Brisson

Cover image: Used with permission of Princeton University Library. Princeton Collections of Papyri AM 4117. Manuscripts Division. Department of Rare Books and Special Collections. Princeton University Library.

Library of Congress Cataloging-in-Publication Data

Batten, Alicia J.
   What are they saying about the letter of James? / Alicia J. Batten.
     p. cm.
   Includes bibliographical references (p.   ).
   ISBN 978-0-8091-4620-8 (alk. paper)
   1. Bible. N.T. James—Criticism, interpretation, etc. I. Title.
   BS2785.52.B38 2009
   227′.9106—dc22

                                     2009013975

Published by Paulist Press
997 Macarthur Boulevard
Mahwah, New Jersey 07430

www.paulistpress.com

Printed and bound in the
United States of America

CONTENTS

ACKNOWLEDGMENTS

First, I would like to thank Lawrence Boadt, CSP, of Paulist Press for accepting my proposal to write this book, as well as project editor James Quigley and Paulist managing editor Paul McMahon. Gratitude goes to members of the Context Group for their ongoing encouragement, and to my new institution back in Canada, the University of Sudbury/Université de Sudbury, for its support. Most of this manuscript was written while teaching at Pacific Lutheran University (PLU), in Tacoma, Washington. PLU generously provided me with a Regency Advancement Award, sabbatical funding, and supported me in obtaining a Graves Award in the Humanities from the American Council of Learned Societies. I will always appreciate the collegiality and professionalism of the members of the Religion Department at PLU and it is with much affection that I dedicate this book to them.

INTRODUCTION

The Letter of James, one of a group of Christian Testament letters often categorized as the Catholic or General Epistles,[1] has received a renaissance of interest in the past thirty years. For centuries, it is fair to say that James, like most of these general letters, was relatively neglected by biblical scholarship, which preferred to focus upon the letters attributed to the apostle Paul and, of course, the gospels. No doubt there is a range of interconnected reasons why James now receives more attention, including developments in biblical scholarship apart from research on the letter itself. Cultural, institutional and theological shifts play significant roles, as do important discoveries about the complexity and diversity of Judaisms and Christianities in the world from which the letter emerged. In addition, and as we will see throughout this book, new approaches to James have shed fresh light on its thematic emphases, its structure and argument as well as questions of who the author and audience may have been.

Analysis of ancient Christian and Jewish literatures, both those within the biblical canon and those without, illustrates that historically, ancient Jews and Christians had a range of expressing and embodying their ideas that shifted under the influence of cultural and social developments. This means that in order to analyze these texts, it is necessary to attend as much to understanding the ancient world as it is to the texts themselves. We will see that many of the authors discussed in this volume do just that, whether it is with regard to writing conventions, moral behavior or social and economic practices. Thus the very process of learning more about an ancient letter such as James enables one to gain a better appreciation of the world of antiquity in general.

What follows are four chapters, each dealing with an area of research on James that has undergone significant development in the past thirty years. We will begin by examining what authors are saying about the genre, structure and rhetoric of the letter. Is this text, for example, truly a letter? Moreover, for decades, many scholars considered James to be a loose assemblage of teachings and traditions with little overall purpose or literary structure. Such a view has generally been rejected, and thus we will explore what patterns and organization writers have uncovered in James. Such insights, in turn, allow contemporary scholars to examine how the text attempts to persuade its audience, or how it is rhetorical. Does it conform to classical Greek configurations of rhetorical arguments, for example? Is it possible to determine an overarching rhetorical structure? These questions have and will continue to receive considerable attention with regard to James.

The subsequent chapter tackles the perennial questions of the authorship and audience of the letter. There never has been consensus on these questions, as even some ancient and medieval commentators questioned whether "James," meaning James of Jerusalem, or James the Just, mentioned by the apostle Paul as "the Lord's brother" (Gal 1:19) and one of the reputed "pillars" (Gal 2:9), was truly the author. Many do not grant that James of Jerusalem was the real author, but there has been a resurgence of interest in this particular figure.[2] Moreover, the text provides only a very vague identification of the audience as "the twelve tribes in the Diaspora" (Jas 1:1). How shall we read the latter phrase: as a figurative designation; or, does it literally refer to Jews living outside of Palestine? Contemporary scholars continue to try to answer these questions.

Next, the book examines what scholars are discussing regarding the various themes found in James. The chapter is divided between theological and moral/social themes although this division is primarily for the purposes of organization because James does not separate these two domains. One area that continues to be of interest and considerable disagreement is the relationship between the ideas found in James with those found in the letters of Paul. Here, scholars continue to have vastly different positions, and thus this topic requires the most development. Other issues include the much studied question of James' attitudes towards poverty and wealth, his understanding of the human being, his attitude towards the Law and a variety of other topics.

The last chapter surveys some of the recent publications on James and the sayings of Jesus. It has long been noticed that the letter shares ideas with those found in the gospels, especially Matthew's Sermon on the Mount, even though James never directly attributes any of these ideas to Jesus. Contemporary scholarship, however, attempts to go beyond listing possible parallels to explaining how James seems to transform these sayings to make them his own. Here, we return to ancient rhetorical practices in particular, for the notion that one could take previous wisdom and alter it to fit a new context was practiced by a variety of writers in antiquity, and could have a persuasive effect. Thus contemporary scholarship attempts to understand how James may be employing this rhetorical technique and to what ends.

By examining one letter, one not only gleans insight about a particular text, but one enters the complicated and enduringly mysterious world of antiquity, in which people had vastly different perspectives and practices from the modern west. One aim of this publication is thus to invite more study of this ancient world, and the literature that it produced. Second, although learning about how little consensus there is on a variety of issues surrounding the Letter of James may be frustrating, I hope that the book will remind readers of how difficult it is to understand these texts, and that moderns cannot presume to facilely "apply" them to contemporary life without serious study and critical thought. This is not to suggest that James is completely incomprehensible, but that it is nonetheless very difficult to understand. Although some interpretations are clearly better than others, there will never be a final definitive interpretation of James, for like all literary texts, it remains, at some level, beyond our grasp. A major goal of the book is therefore to provide some introductory material that is sufficiently intriguing such that it provokes the reader to explore some of the issues around and themes within the letter of James more thoroughly. *What Are They Saying About the Letter of James?* is intended as an entryway to further reading and study.

1
GENRE, STRUCTURE AND RHETORIC OF JAMES

In the past thirty years, the Letter of James has been subject to a range of analyses manifesting a variety of proposals as to its genre, structure and rhetoric. Although there is no consensus on any of these issues, the discussion has been lively and is ongoing, for such form-critical and rhetorical matters are important to understanding other dimensions of the letter. For example, if we have a clearer grasp of what James is attempting to argue, then we are better able to posit possible social locations and concerns of both the author and audience. Thus it is appropriate to begin this book with a survey of scholarship on these issues, as it forms a requisite backdrop for entering into other questions about the Letter of James.

The Genre of James

Although James is casually referred to as a "letter," it was not considered as such by modern critical scholarship until relatively recently. This is largely due to the influential commentary by Martin Dibelius, published in German in 1921, with the first English translation appearing in 1976. Dibelius classified James as *paraenesis*, meaning that it consisted of ethical admonitions loosely strung together, often only by catchwords, with no overall integrating idea or theme. Dibelius understood *paraenesis* to contain purely traditional materials and to be very general, not directed to any single recipient or addressing any concrete situation. As paraenesis, James lacked an "epistolary situation," and the only clear "letter" characteristic of James was its prescript in James 1:1.[1] This is not to say that Dibelius deemed James to be of little interest for the study of Christian origins. On the contrary, he thought that James was a witness to a period of early Christianity in which eschatological fervor had diminished, as the letter's ethical content shows that moral teaching was developing within the primitive church. However, the classification of James as paraenesis had consequences in that no specific audience for the text could be proposed, nor did Dibelius think that James had a particular theology.

Dibelius's work was of such significance that current scholars rarely write about James without engaging his commentary. Yet some major shifts in thinking about the genre of James have emerged. First, the definition of *paraenesis* has been revisited. For example, Leo G. Perdue's studies of the concept indicate that it can indeed address a specific audience and have a socializing purpose.[2] Others, such as Peter H. Davids, argue that *paraenesis* can have rhetorical aims, and attempt to promote a particular point of view for a concrete situation.[3] This means that even if one continues to classify James as *paraenesis*, one need not accept all of Dibelius's conclusions about the intent and nature of the genre. James could contain an overall argument and possess theological coherence and still be understood primarily as paraenesis. Moreover, although Davids granted that James contained many traditional materials, he thought that they had been crafted to serve particular purposes in the letter. As he writes, "scholarship must move beyond Dibelius' form-critical view of James, valuable as that is, and discover the redactional level."[4]

Other scholars, such as Ernst Baasland[5] and Patrick J. Hartin,[6] distinguish *paraenesis* from *protrepsis* and classify James as the latter. Hartin, building upon the work of John G. Gammie,[7] understands *protrepsis* to contain more sustained arguments than *paraenesis*, and thinks, as Baasland does, that James is artfully arranged to reflect sustained arguments. However, it is not clear whether the ancients distinguished paraenesis from protrepsis, and even whether paraenesis is a *type* of literature. David Hutchinson Edgar, for example, thinks that "the term *paraenesis*, as demonstrated by its supposed representatives, is too vague to function effectively as a definite *genre;* rather, it could at best serve to describe the *function* of certain texts."[8] Wesley Hiram Wachob also rejects the application of paraenesis as a literary genre to James, instead arguing that paraenesis is simply a "mode of persuasion or argument," and James is best understood as deliberative rhetoric, that is, rhetoric that seeks to persuade an audience to future action.[9] Furthermore, Wiard Popkes's discussion of James and paraenesis concludes that "James is not a *paraenesis* in an undifferentiated, one sided meaning of the term" but that the letter does serve many paraenetic functions and has "paraenetic character."[10] Thus it is fair to say that overall, the acceptance of Dibelius's *particular understanding* of *paraenesis* and its application as a *literary genre* to James has been either rejected or seriously revised by those working on the text in the past three decades.

Similarly, considerable rethinking has been done on the question of whether or not James can be called a letter and if so, what kind of letter? Study of ancient epistolography has shown that there was great variety among letter forms in antiquity. A variety of literature could be classified as letters, and as David Aune indicates, epistolary postscripts and prescripts could "frame almost any type of composition" including "letter-essays, philosophical letters, and novelistic and fictional letters."[11]

A significant study that paved the way for the discussion of James as a letter is a 1970 article by Fred O. Francis, which focuses on the beginnings and endings of James and 1 John.[12] Francis argues that James bears resemblance to *secondary letters,* or *literary letters,* such as the ones found within the writings of the first-century Jewish historian Josephus (*Antiquities* 8.50–54). They possess double opening statements, as James does, and end abruptly, with no epistolary close, also a characteristic of James. Such features appear in Hellenistic private and public letters,[13] and some letters leave out greetings and closing salutations altogether.[14] Thus for Francis, "James and 1 John may be understood as epistles from start to finish—secondary epistles in form and literary treatment of their subject matter."[15]

Building largely upon the work of Francis, commentators began treating James as a letter, replete with an organizational structure and coherent argument. In his 1997 book, Manabu Tsuji claims that not only is James a letter based upon its opening and closing, but that its content conforms most closely to the tradition of Jewish Diaspora letters—letters that seek to unify Jews in the Diaspora with those at home and that provide a means for Diaspora Jews (although for Tsuji, James's audience is Christian) to cope with their situation.[16] Karl-Wilhelm Niebuhr similarly classifies James as this type of literature, with its address to the "twelve tribes in the diaspora" indicating its similarity to ancient Jewish Diaspora letters, such as those found in 2 Maccabees (2 Macc 1:1–9; 1:10—2:18) and the *Letter of Jeremiah,* among others.[17] Peter Davids, who in his 1982 commentary was one of the first after Francis to treat James as a structured letter, has recently concurred with Niebuhr's conclusions about James as a Jewish Diaspora letter, pointing out that if James belongs to such a literary tradition, it is evidence of a possible Palestinian provenance.[18]

Not all agree that James is a letter, however. Most recently S. R. Llewellyn has argued that the prescript of James (1:1) was a later addition to a text that was essentially a collection of paraenetic materials. Llewellyn likens James to collections of sayings such as the sayings source Q and the *Gospel of Thomas.*[19] However, even if Llewellyn is correct about the tacking on of 1:1, the comparison of James to Q and Thomas does not exempt James from structural and rhetorical analysis, but makes the case for it even stronger given that Q and Thomas are not rhetorically unsophisticated.

What can we conclude from this brief discussion of the genre of James? First, it is clear that despite the many contributions of Dibelius, his conclusions about James as paraenesis are no longer generally accepted. Even those who would still classify James as paraenesis do not think that James lacks structure and coherence. Indeed, rhetorical studies of James are now flourishing, as we will see further on. Second, Francis's seminal article on the structure of James, which we will also explore in more detail directly, has paved the way for the analysis of James as a literary letter, but a letter nonetheless even though Francis did not think that a specific audience could be determined.[20] His work has helped scholars to see parallels between James and other letter traditions, most notably Jewish Diaspora letters. Although there is still no consensus on the overall genre of James, authors no longer view it as a loose jumble of teachings held together, at best, by catchwords.

The Structure of James

As mentioned, Francis's article on James and 1 John paved the way, in many respects, for the renewed analysis of the structure of James. This is not to say that earlier scholars paid no attention to James's structure—they did—but their work was largely overshadowed by that of Dibelius.[21]

Francis perceived a twofold structure in the opening chapter of James: James 1:2–11 and James 1:12–25, which in turn, introduces some major themes in the letter as a whole. Each of these sections begins with "technical liturgical-epistolary terms for 'joy' and 'blessedness.'"[22] Within this chapter the text repeats the emphases of testing/steadfastness (Jas 1:2–4; 12–18), wisdom-words/reproaching (1:5–8; 19–21) and rich-poor/doers (1:9–11; 22–25). This introductory section is followed by 1:26–27, a "literary hinge" that both recapitulates the introduction and prepares the reader for the main arguments in the body of the letter, namely faith and how one behaves towards the rich and the poor (Jas 2:1–26) and the "angry passion of wisdom, words, and position."[23] Moreover, the thematic pattern of testing, wisdom and rich-poor/doers that is repeated (A B C/A B C) in the introduction is inversed throughout the body of the epistle (rich-poor/doers in 2:1–26 [C]; wisdom/words in 3:1—5:6 [B]; and the theme of testing/steadfastness underlying the whole thing [A]), thereby forming a smooth transition between the recapitulation in 1:26–27 to the discussion of rich-poor/doers and forming a chiasm or chiasmus (a reverse parallelism) throughout the letter as a whole. James 5:7–11 forms an epistolary eschatological close while 5:12–20, although abrupt, is a perfectly acceptable manner of closing as illustrated by Hellenistic letters that "just stop."[24] Moreover, this closing is thematically related to the warning about being deceived by the source of adversity in James 1:16 with its concern for those facing adversity in 5:13–18 and "those who are deceived" in 5:19–20.[25] A final phrase that often appears in Hellenistic letters is *pro pantōn* ("above all" Jas 5:12) and an oath formula (Jas 5:12) is also typically found in closing sections of such letters. Finally, the reference to prayer is "an established element of the epistolary close of the NT epistles"[26] and thus James conforms quite well to this close in 5:13–18.

Davids came to some similar conclusions as Francis about the structure of James, although independently and "without Francis' theoretical foundation."[27] He concurred that there was a twofold structure in the introductory chapter that repeats the three themes of testing, wisdom and poverty excelling over wealth, with the second section (1:12–27) developing these themes in greater detail and connecting the wisdom theme to the discussion of speech. Then Davids argued for a giant chiasm in the body of the epistle (Jas 2:1—5:6) insofar as it inverts the three themes with a discussion of poverty and wealth (Jas 2:1–26), the call for pure speech that comes from wisdom (3:1-4:12) and an emphasis upon testing through wealth (4:13—5:6).[28] The final section of the letter (5:7–20) consists of the things already identified by Francis: eschatological exhortation, thematic reprise and normal closing topics and formulas such as *pro pantōn*, an oath formula and a health wish that emphasizes prayer.[29] Thus James is a literary letter that manifests a clear structure and ends in a manner consistent with literary as well as some early Christian letters.

The notion that James is a chiasm in its entirety has been supported by various other scholars as well. James Reese, for example, has argued for an A, B, C, B′, A′ structure. A (1:2–27) focuses upon testing, prayerful seeking of wisdom and acts of maturity; B (2:1–26) is a sermon that warns against relying upon the rich; and C (3:1–18) is the heart of the letter that exhorts community leaders about the "terrifying" responsibility of teacher and sage.[30] Warnings against the rich follow in B′ (4:1—5:6) and the closing, A′ (5:7–20), again exhorts the audience on the subjects of testing, prayer and mature action. Thus for Reese, 3:1–18 is the center of the letter both structurally and thematically. More recently, Robert B. Crotty proposes that James 4:1–3 reflects the central issue of the letter with, as he interprets it, its stress upon "the human person as battlefield."[31] For Crotty, the letter is framed by the inclusio of James 1:16–18 and James 5:19–20 and works inward from these two limits, offering positive and negative options from which the audience must choose.

In his 1991 book, Patrick Hartin describes a structure for James that reflects a chiastic pattern within the body of the epistle (Jas 2:1 –5:6). Here Hartin argues that the theme of rich and poor includes the entire section (2:1–13; 5:1–6), then, moving inward, James focuses upon faith and action (2:14–26; 4:13–17), then speech and the tongue (3:1–12; 4:11–12), and finally, at the "heart of the parallel structures," is the theme of wisdom (3:13–18; 4:1–10).[32] Indeed for Hartin, James is a clear example of wisdom literature. Although he does not describe these parallel sections with so much detail in his 2003 commentary, Hartin indicates that he roughly follows the same structure identified in the 1991 book.[33] James 1:1–27 comprises the introduction to the letter, establishing five themes that will be expanded upon later in the text: the testing of faith; the gift of wisdom; rich and poor; control of speech; and being doers of the word.[34] The body of the letter then consists of six sections, some of which begin with markers such as *adelphoi* ("brothers" 2:1, 14; 3:1; 4:11; 5:7, 12) and *Age nun* ("come now" 4:13; 5:1). Thus 2:1–13 focuses upon not showing favoritism; 2:14–26 emphasizes faith and works; 3:1–12 discusses the tongue and speech; 3:13—4:10 consists of a call to friendship with God; 4:11–12 warns against speaking evil; and 4:13—5:6 passes judgment on the rich because of their friendship with the world. James 5:7–20 forms the conclusion of the letter with its emphasis upon prayer comparable to the endings of 1 John and Jude.[35] Although he grants that James does not show a systematically developed theology, Hartin does think that James manifests clear theological themes, as we shall see later on, especially as they pertain to how humans should conduct themselves.

The view that James reflects chiastic patterns is not universally agreed upon. Moreover, as we have seen, scholars who argue for chiastic structures in the letter disagree on where and how the chiasm manifests itself, and what the center of the chiasm is. As Mark Taylor has observed, "some chiastic proposals appear strained in order to fit a preconceived pattern."[36] Thus many recent studies of James's structure do not argue for particular chiastic patterns at all, but for more thematic structuring principles.

For example, even though Luke Timothy Johnson's commentary does not reject outright the possibility of chiasms in James, for indeed "chiasm happens as much by accident as by design,"[37] he does not focus upon such patterns as important for its structure. For Johnson, James 1:1–27 serves as a table of contents or *epitome* of the entire letter as it introduces topics that are further elaborated upon in the essays embedded in James 5 2:1—5:18. For example, the inversion of rich and poor in 1:9–10 is further developed by 2:1–7 and 4:13—5:6. Throughout the commentary, Johnson discusses each unit in James as both a thematic and literary segment, paying particular attention to Hellenistic *topoi* or themes such as "envy" in 3:13—4:10, as well as to conventions of ancient rhetoric. Thus for Johnson, James is a coherent letter wherein the introductory chapter prepares the audience for the work as a whole. Moreover, he sees a " 'deep structure' of polar opposition between 'friendship with the world' and 'friendship with God' " as governing the inclusion and overall arrangement of James's materials.[38]

This perception that James exhibits a deep structure appears in the work of Timothy Cargal, who takes a very different approach, that of structural semiotics as developed by Greimas, to the letter. Cargal argues that James must be examined not at the level of syntax, but at the semantic or "meaning" level.[39] He divides James into four sections—1:1–21; 1:22—2:26; 3:1—4:12; and 4:11—5:20—arguing that each segment offers examples of positive and negative behavior. The introductory identification of the twelve tribes in the "dispersion" with the concluding reference to bringing back those who wander from the truth functions as an *inclusio*, which in light of the rest of the letter serves to "restore" the audience to the convictions that the author sets forth. The audience of James is to understand itself as this metaphorical dispersion that has drifted from the truth and must be restored and brought home. Thus, while Cargal does not apply ancient rhetorical or epistolary frameworks to James, he does understand it to be an organized and coherent letter, for which the introduction serves an important purpose.

In his "canonical" approach to James, Robert Wall adopts Cargal's metaphorical reading of James's reference to the twelve tribes in the Diaspora as an address to "every immature believer who has 'scattered' from the truth."[40] Wall focuses upon James as a text within the Christian canon and as such, he looks to understand James's meaning for the contemporary reader as opposed to the original audience. This means that he does not focus on as many of the precise historical questions surrounding the letter as many other scholars do. He does, however, concur that James is a structured and rhetorical document and places special emphasis upon two opening thesis statements, James 1:2–11 and 1:12–21, that introduce the "composition's theological calculus."[41] For Wall, James is written to an audience whose faith in God is threatened by everyday trials. The addressees thus must make a choice to remain faithful to God—be a "community of the wise"—and receive promised blessings in the future, or to blame God for the community's troubles, to be deceived and to forfeit the " 'crown of life' that is the blessing of all those who endure."[42] The main body of the letter (1:22—5:6) is then a "commentary" on the wisdom from above, wisdom being the central focus of the text. The concluding section (5:7–20) then forms an *inclusio* for the letter as it provides the motivation for why the audience should follow the letter's teachings: "the coming of the Lord is near."[43] The final exhortations take on an urgency given the eschatological judgment, and the audience is especially exhorted to bring back those who have strayed from the path of wisdom.

A focus on eschatology characterizes Todd Penner's study of James. He argues that 1:2–12 and 4:6—5:12 form an eschatological *inclusio* to the letter. For Penner, as for most scholars of James, James 1:1 is the epistolary greeting; then the body is introduced by 1:2–12 with the body proper in 1:13—4:5 and the body's conclusion in 4:6—5:12, with 5:13–20 as the letter's epistolary conclusion.[44] James 1:2–12 is the introduction because first, it evidences a deliberate chiastic structure of 1:2–4 (testing of the believer = A), 1:5–11 (two themes of wisdom and reversal relating to the believer = B) and 1:12 (testing of the believer again = A); and second, it contains words and "leitmotifs" that appear in James's closing and throughout the letter as a whole.[45] The conclusion to the body also possesses a chiasm consisting of 4:6–12 (injunctions to the community = A), 4:13—5:6 (indictment of the rich/proud = B) and 5:7–12 (injunctions to the community = A).[46] Motifs throughout this *inclusio* come from Old Testament prophetic literature, but here, appear in an "explicitly Christian eschatological context."[47] Through his analysis of the textual shifts and thematic parallels in the two sections, Penner concludes that the eschatological framework functions as motivation for the audience to adopt James's ethical teachings and provides a theological context for understanding the letter as a whole.

Other thematic approaches to James also indicate to what extent the opening verses identify a key idea or ideas that shape the structure of the text. François Vouga advocates the topic of "faith" as central to James, emphasizing the role of the opening statement in James 1:2–4. Vouga divides James into three main parts, all of which begin with the theme of faith: 1:2–19a; 2:19b—3:18; and 4:1—5:20.[48] Ralph Martin adopts Vouga's tripartite structure, but offers a more detailed subdivision of each section, and states that chapter 1 "holds the key to the letter's structure and sets out the basic issues to be faced: how is human existence to fulfill its goal and find its dignity?"[49] James B. Adamson thinks that the first chapter of the letter, with its focus upon "the Christian mind" in 1:2–18 and "Christian conduct" in 1:19–27, is the source of every other theme in the rest of the letter.[50] Martin Klein understands James 1:2–27 as an expression of both the theme ("perfect work" [Jas 1:4] understood by Klein as the testing of faith in daily life) and its manifestation in lived existence. He argues that the rest of the letter either further elaborates upon this theme or provides practical examples of how it can be achieved.[51] Although he grants less deliberate structure to James than other scholars, Richard Bauckham argues that James 1:2–27 introduces every topic developed throughout the rest of the letter. Moreover, Bauckham says that the first chapter of James "is designed to highlight the overarching theme of the whole work: 'perfection.' "[52]

Finally, some recent approaches to James have not focused on theme, but applied other methods to the study of James's structure. Kenneth D. Tollefson says that the "compiler" of the letter uses dialectical discourse or binary opposition, which dates back to early Greek literature, and is sometimes characteristic of oral cultures. He works through the letter arguing that James incorporates a sequence of thesis/antithesis/synthesis on a range of topics, as well as imperatives and familial images, to aid the audience in building group maturity or perfection, which is accomplished through critical choices, changes in behavior and God's grace.[53] Mark E. Taylor applies textlinguistic analysis to James, which highlights the role of various *inclusios* throughout the letter. In particular, the *inclusio* that Taylor (and others) see in James 1:2–4/1:12 and 1:12/1:25 supports the notion that 1:2–25 functions as an important introduction to the letter. This focus on *inclusios* also draws Taylor to a reexamination of the function of the Old Testament quotations and allusions, specifically Leviticus 19:18, Deuteronomy 6 and Proverbs 3:34, within the structure of James. These references figure importantly within the *inclusios* that Taylor sees, and thus he points out that their role as well as the manner in which James appropriates other texts "might be an important key to the riddle of James's structure."[54]

Although there is no consensus whatsoever about the structure of James, Dibelius's claim that the text is a loose string of sayings with minimal coherence is no longer upheld by the majority of scholars. James is generally understood to be an ordered letter. For some of the authors identified above, attention to structure has been especially significant for identifying the central theme or themes of James. Although not all agree that James is shaped by a particular epistolary structure,[55] by and large, scholars identify the introduction of James (although they disagree about its precise parameters) as important for identifying what will be developed further in the letter. Moreover, there is considerable agreement that 5:7–20 (again, the specific boundaries are disputed) functions well as a closing. There is increasing consensus that between these two frames, James contains structured arguments or essays. Thus we turn to a discussion of the role of rhetoric in James.

Rhetoric and James

Effectively convincing an audience that it should change its behavior, resume prior practices or come to a specific judgment about an issue or person was a great skill in the Greco-Roman world. Thus, if one were fortunate enough to receive an education, one was taught the art of persuasion, or rhetoric, especially as it pertained to oral communication. We cannot read texts from the first-century Mediterranean basin without considering what roles rhetorical skills and practices may have played in their creation. This is not to say that all texts from the first century were influenced by rhetorical practices, but given the pervasive presence of rhetoric at this time, one must at least consider its potential sway on the production of a text. As Burton L. Mack writes:

> All people, whether formally trained or not, were fully schooled in the wily ways of sophists, the eloquence required at civic festivals, the measured tones of the local teacher, and the heated debates where differences of opinion battled for the right to say what should be done. To be engulfed in the culture of Hellenism meant to have ears trained for the rhetoric of speech. Rhetoric provided the rules for making critical judgments in the course of all forms of social intercourse. Early Christians were not unskilled, either as critics of their cultures of context or as proponents of their own emerging persuasions.[56]

Some contemporary scholars object that because ancient rhetorical theory developed separately from epistolary theory, those New Testament texts which qualify as letters may not have been affected by rhetoric in the manner that others assume.[57] However, as the quotation from Mack makes clear, one did not require formal training in rhetorical theory in order to come under its influence. Rhetoric was part of the air that one breathed, at least in the cities. Moreover, as Aune indicates, by the third century BCE, rhetoric had come to affect letter writing.[58]

Rhetorical studies of ancient texts are important because they aid in reconstructing, or at least positing, a possible scenario to which the text addresses itself. Put another way, the examination of a text's argument and what it seeks to do enables one to imagine the situation of the text's audience. This situation, deemed the "rhetorical situation" by Lloyd Bitzer, need not be identical to the audience's exact historical circumstances, but the two can overlap.[59] In attempting to reconstruct a rhetorical situation, one attends to the exigency or problem that needs correction, the audience that is capable of being influenced and the rhetorical constraints or "beliefs, attitudes, documents, facts, traditions, images, interests, motives and the like."[60] The precise historical situation of the audience is not envisaged, but rather, the circumstances or ideologies that the writer is attempting to address, which quite likely relate to the real situation of some people at that time, or at least to the text's author's perception of what some were experiencing and believing.

In the early twentieth century, some scholars incorporated Greek rhetorical practices into their respective examinations of James,[61] but such studies dwindled until relatively recently. Indeed Dibelius recognized many rhetorical elements in his commentary, such as alliteration (e.g., Jas 1:2), parechesis (when words of different derivation sound similar) (e.g., Jas 1:24) and rhyming (e.g., Jas 1:6), all of which he deemed intentional. All scholars maintain, moreover, that James is written in high-quality *Koine* (common) Greek. Clearly this was an author of considerable skill who wanted to convey a particular message to the audience. Hence, the seeming contradiction between a sophisticated use of language and the notion that James is a loose jumble of sayings is puzzling. As Finnish scholar Lauri Thurén indicates, since the letter evidences "a good command of grammar, and many stylistic devices typical of contemporary rhetoric are frequently used, it would be unnatural if the author lacked a clear message or disregarded elementary requirements for organizing his speech."[62] One would think that given the facility with the Greek language exhibited by the letter, the author would also have the ability to organize the contents in a lucid manner.

Before delving into some specific rhetorical studies, it is important to point out that generally, scholars who attribute rhetorical argumentative strategies to James consider it to be an example of deliberative rhetoric, which, as mentioned earlier, is rhetoric that seeks to persuade the audience to some sort of action in the future. Aristotle explains this *species* of rhetoric in the third chapter of his treatise, *On Rhetoric*. Other *species* include epideictic, which takes the form of praise or blame, and judicial, which asks the audience to judge something from the past.[63] One exception to the view that James is primarily deliberative is the work of Thurén, who certainly grants that there are many deliberative segments, but also notices some minor judicial sections (e.g., Jas 5:1–6), and indicates that the text seeks to reinforce some of the existing values of the audience, and thus could be understood as epideictic in a vague sense.[64] He thus assesses James as a mix of *species*, noting, as well, that determining clear differences between epideictic and deliberative rhetoric is often open to interpretation.

Especially significant for contemporary rhetorical analyses of James has been Wilhelm Wuellner's lengthy article in *Linguistica Biblica*.[65] Here, Wuellner applies insights from recent studies of rhetoric as well as semiotics and communication theory in order to understand the argument and genre of the letter, as well as the situation of the reader or audience. He does not focus on historical questions, but on textual ones, arguing that James must be understood as an unfolding argument that develops as it progresses within both its social setting and the pragmatic relations within the text itself (*Textpragmatik*).[66] He divides James into an introduction (1:1–12) which includes the address and greetings, and reference to a central theme of the letter, or *exordium* (1:2–4). A crucial function of the *exordium* is not only to introduce ideas that will be addressed later, but to establish an *ethos*, or authority, of the speaker, and a climate of *pathos* or feeling that will engage the audience and predispose it to listen.[67] This *exordium* is followed by a series of positive and negative contrasts that state the facts (*narratio*) (1:5–12).[68] This iteration of "facts" is important as it prompts the reason for the speech.[69] The latter section also contains a *propositio* or main point that the text wants to convey. For

Wuellner, this appears in James 1:12 where the text announces a blessing upon those who endure trial and who will receive a "crown of life" that God has promised to those who love God.[70] The body of the letter, or *argumentatio*, provides support for the *propositio* and consists of James 1:13—5:6 and is characterized by a series of six "speech sections" (*Redeabschnitt*) that again contain pairs of positive and negative behaviors. James 5:7–20 is the conclusion or *peroratio* and parallels some of the ideas in the introduction (specifically 5:7–8 is a *recapitulatio* that "recaps" earlier themes).[71] The *peroratio* conventionally recalls ideas from earlier in a speech in order to remind the audience, and can also include some concrete exhortation for living, which the end of James certainly does with its emphasis upon prayer and bringing back those who wander from the truth. Thus the introduction and conclusion form an *inclusio* around the *argumentatio*. Wuellner argues that James is a very practical text; it is not so much teaching the readers/listeners new ideas as it is recruiting them to a particular plan of action.

Wuellner's particular combination of methodologies has not been widely adopted, yet his work has significantly "reinvigorated" the rhetorical analysis of James. John H. Elliott, for example, adopts Wuellner's rhetorical structure of James (with some modifications), particularly the emphasis on the positive and negative behaviors that Wuellner identifies in the body of the letter. Elliott's work does not delve into the rhetorical structure and details of James very much, but situates the main argument within the larger social and cultural world of the ancient Mediterranean, with special attention to issues of purity and pollution. He argues that James's central message of wholeness and unity at the personal, social and cosmic levels emerges throughout the letter through the systematic contrasts between negative assessments and positive exhortations. James "employs notions of purity and pollution to undergird an ethic of holy nonconformity" in a unified and coherent manner.[72]

Ernst Baasland concurs with Wuellner regarding the *peroratio* of James (Jas 5:7–20) but otherwise outlines a different rhetorical structure. According to Baasland, following the *exordium* (1:2–15) James contains two *propositios*: James 1:16–22, which is elaborated by 1:23–27 and followed by an *argumentatio* in James 2:1—3:12; and then another *propositio* in James 3:13–18, elaborated by 4:1–6 and followed by an *argumentatio* in 4:7—5:6.[73] Consistent with others' findings, Baasland thinks that the beginning and ending of James parallel each other thematically, with their references to remaining steadfast and warnings against wandering from the truth (Jas 1:16 and Jas 5:19).[74]

Hubert Frankenmölle also considers 5:7–20 to be the *peroratio* while James 1:2–18 forms the *exordium*.[75] As many have already noted, these two "ends" of James form an *inclusio* that frames the letter. Moreover, Frankenmölle agrees that the *exordium* introduces key themes of the letter that are developed later. He states that the main thesis (*Grundthese*) of the letter is in James 1:4 with its emphasis upon becoming perfect or complete through testing and steadfastness. The exhortation to be complete reappears in 1:19–27 and 3:1–2. Deficiency in wisdom (1:5) is readdressed in 3:13–18, deficiency in faith (1:6–8) in 2:14–26 and deficiency in the self understanding of rich and poor (1:9–11) in 2:1–13 and 5:1–6. Moreover, James 1:13–15 stresses the temptation of submitting to one's desire while 1:16–18 reminds the audience that God is the foundation for Christian existence. These ideas are connected to James 4:1–12, which stresses humility before God.[76]

Thurén joins Frankenmölle in his understanding of the *exordium* (1:2–18) and *peroratio* (5:7–20), noting the parallels between the two. The *propositio* of James lies, however, in 1:19–27 wherein there lies the stress on consistency between faith and action.[77] This idea is supported by the *argumentatio* (2:1—5:6), which Thurén divides into three parts: action/money (2:1–26); speech/wisdom (3:1—4:12); and speech and action/money (4:13—5:6). This section supports the *propositio* of the letter because each section refers to the relationship between "principle and practice, words and deeds, conviction and action."[78] The themes in these sections also relate to ideas in the *exordium* and *peroratio* of the letter. Thurén also states that given the direct and frank tone of James (it has been observed that James "barks" on occasion!), the author must be very aware of the audience's situation and have a close relationship with the audience. Thurén does not, however, attempt to reconstruct what this situation might be.

Above we have explored a representative selection of scholarship that seeks to determine the rhetorical structure of the letter *as a whole*. Not all scholars are convinced that such an overall structure can be determined for James, or at least, they have not attempted to perform such an analysis. A number of studies simply focus upon a section, or a particular characteristic of James's rhetoric. For example, Hartin addresses rhetorical patterns and devices within sections of the letter in his recent commentary. He argues, for example, that James often follows the "elaboration of a theme" exercise that one finds in rhetorical handbooks of antiquity. Such an exercise presents a theme or topic, provides a reason why the idea deserves support, and subsequently a proof and embellishment (that can often appeal to some sort of authority) and finally, a conclusion.[79] J. D. N. van der Westhuizen examines how particular stylistic techniques, common in Hellenistic rhetoric, function in James 2:14–26 to meet the rhetorical situation. He argues that the passage uses a variety of tools in its overall arrangement and style to produce a logical argument in order to persuade those who "profess to have faith [but] who neglect to do what the author feels the Christian should do."[80]

Duane Watson, an expert in rhetorical analysis of the New Testament, has produced two close analyses of sections of James in light of Greco-Roman rhetorical techniques. In one study he argues that James 2 is deliberative rhetoric and takes the form of a classical elaboration of a theme exercise, incorporating aspects of what is known as a diatribe.[81] The diatribe is an ancient pedagogical technique that many ancient authors, including the apostle Paul (e.g., Romans 3), incorporate into their texts. This technique does not follow a rigid structure, but is generally characterized by direct address to the audience, and the introduction of an imaginary discussion partner or interlocutor with whom the speaker has a debate. Thus diatribes often contain many questions and answers, sometimes with the speaker "posing absurdities which the interlocutor must strongly reject."[82] Watson argues that James employs the diatribe in chapter 2 to augment the argument. Although one cannot reconstruct the actual historical situation that James may be attempting to address with this section, particularly whether the scenario of a rich man and a poor man entering an assembly actually took place, the "fact that James addresses the problem of faith without works makes it likely that this was a perceived problem."[83] Watson's other article examines James 3:1–12, and contends, *contra* Dibelius, that this section is a "unified composition, constructed according to a standard elaboration pattern for argumentation discussed by Greco-Roman rhetorical works."[84] Dibelius thought that this section of James had no unity, the ideas bumping and clashing with one another.[85] Watson systematically works through the section, illustrating how it conforms to a classical pattern of elaboration. In this case, the *propositio* of James 3:1a ("Let not many of you become teachers") is supported by a reason (*ratio*) in James 3:1b, corroboration (*confirmatio*) in 3:2, confirmation (*exornatio*) in 3:3–10a and conclusion in 3:10–12 (*conplexio*). In a more recent study, however, Watson indicates that he does not see a clear rhetorical structure in the letter as a whole,[86] even though he clearly grants, as we have seen, that James employs classical patterns of argumentation within sections of the letter.

Richard Bauckham takes a similar approach to the structure of James as a whole, stating that the failure to reach a consensus about the overarching argument of James, even when the same methods are used, suggests that something must be wrong. He is critical of those who attempt to do a rhetorical analysis of the entire letter:

> [T]hey have sought a structure which corresponds to some of overall continuity of thought, something approaching a sequential argument progressing through

James. This is the mistake, in my view, made by recent attempts to solve the problem of the structure of James by the application of rhetorical criticism....[87]

Bauckham endorses the work of Watson and others, however, who evaluate smaller units of James according to the rhetorical constraints of antiquity, and thus he is by no means returning to Dibelius's assessment of the text. One of the chief contributions of Bauckham's book, moreover, is his discussion of how James alludes to teachings of Jesus without attribution and in new forms. He compares James to wisdom authors, especially Ben Sira, who passes on preexistent wisdom instruction, but in different words and contexts, thereby making it the wisdom teacher's own.[88] Bauckham's work here is very important, for it provides a literary precedent within wisdom literature, to which James is often compared, for the practice of restating wisdom teachings without crediting the original author. We will return to Bauckham's insights on this matter in a later chapter.

Another recent and significant study involving James and rhetoric is Wesley Hiram Wachob's book, *The Voice of Jesus in the Social Rhetoric of James.* Wachob focuses upon James 2:1–13, arguing, like Watson, that it conforms to the elaboration of a theme exercise explained in Pseudo-Cicero's *Rhetorica ad Herennium.* Here the main theme is stated in James 2:1, interpreted by Wachob to mean that acts of partiality are contrary to the "faith of Jesus Christ."[89] What follows is the reason (*ratio*) in 2:2–4, which provides a "social example" showing how those who show partiality are actually judging others.[90] James includes in his proof a restatement of the first beatitude ("Blessed are the poor" Q 6:20b) in James 2:5, with the assumption that the audience would have recognized this as a teaching of Jesus. In restating the teaching in this way and in the specific context of James 2:1–13, James is attempting to show that Jesus' faith (Jas 2:1) and acts of partiality are "contrary and incompatible."[91] Those, like Jesus, who are "rich in faith" (Jas 2:5) do not judge and do not show partiality. James provides more social examples in 2:6–7, then turns to an argument from written law by invoking the scriptural authority of Leviticus 19:18 in James 2:8–9. Leviticus 19:18 was known as a summary of the Jewish Law in first-century Judaism and thus it is effective here as it shows that if one shows partiality, one is actually violating the entire Law (Jas 2:10). This is confirmed by 2:11. The argument is concluded by 2:12–13, which summarizes the argument and appeals to the emotions through a reference to the coming judgment.

Wachob's work on James 2 is significant for not only does it provide a detailed rhetorical analysis of the unit, it explores how scripture and teachings of Jesus are effectively integrated into the argument. In particular, Wachob shows how James uses the practice of "recitation" whereby students in antiquity would learn to "recite" antecedent texts either verbatim or with different words.[92] Thus such a practice was not confined to the Jewish sages, such as Ben Sira, but is attested in a variety of texts in the Greco-Roman world. Others are building upon Wachob's work,[93] including John S. Kloppenborg, who examines James's reception of Jesus traditions, particularly in James 2:5. Kloppenborg concurs with Wachob that this is a recitation of a Jesus saying, but goes on to demonstrate how James's particular way of reciting the Jesus saying not only underscores how acts of partiality violate Torah, but is actually against the audience's own self-interests insofar as they *are* the poor. As Kloppenborg puts it:

> James' elaboration of Q's bare *hoi ptōchoi* ["the poor"] as *hoi ptōchoi tō kosmō* ["the poor in the world"] makes it clear that these "poor" are aligned with one of the main binary oppositions of the letter, between the (actual) rich and (actual) poor.…James' expansion of Q 6,20b is a function of his need to cement the identification of the addressees with the "poor" of Q 6, 20b.[94]

The letter's readers or hearers will not only appreciate how James had adapted a teaching of Jesus to suit his own purposes, and be impressed by how much James's *ethos* is in line with that of Jesus, they will also see how committing acts of partiality violates their own interests insofar as *they are the poor* who are heirs of God's kingdom.[95]

We will return to James's use of Jesus traditions in a later chapter, but as this brief survey of several scholars' work has shown, James does not blindly integrate earlier traditions, whether they are teachings of Jesus or Jewish scriptures, into his composition.

Conclusion

It may seem that the examination of James's structure and rhetoric is in a bit of a quagmire, as no overall consensus has emerged in the past three decades. Yet, there are some majority views that span European and North American scholarship. For example, James is now understood to be a more structured and rhetorically sophisticated text than Dibelius believed. Considerable agreement has also developed over the role of the introduction of James as a mini "table of contents" to the letter, although the parameters of the introduction and its particular shape remain in some dispute. More agreement exists about the conclusion of the letter, with the majority of scholars granting 5:7–20 as a reasonable and logical way to end the text.

As we have seen regarding James and rhetoric, some authors see an overall rhetorical structure, while others think it can only be found in smaller sections. Several scholars deem James 2:1–13 to be a complete argument that conforms to the classical elaboration of a theme exercise,[96] and Hartin joins Watson in the same assessment of James 3:1–12.[97] Although rhetorical approaches to James do not enable scholars to determine the definitive and concrete historical situation that James's audience was facing, they do raise the question of what sort of rhetorical situation James thought he was addressing. This "situation" is not from Mars, but relates, at some level, to the historical circumstances of the person or people who both produced and received the letter. Thus in the following chapter we will turn to a discussion not only of the author, but the possible recipients of the letter, and observe what authors are currently saying about these issues. Then in chapter 4 we will address what current authors are saying about thematic issues in James, which will also involve attention to the recipients' social realities.

2
AUTHORSHIP AND AUDIENCE OF JAMES

Just as debates about the literary and rhetorical structure of James remain energetic, the question of who wrote the letter is far from resolved. Certainly, the text *says* it is by a specific person, James (Jas 1:1), but who is this James? Today, there are scholars who uphold that the letter was written by James the Just, a significant figure in the early church. However, many other authors argue that despite the claim to be by James, the text was not truly produced by him. This chapter will therefore explore the reasons for these differing views.

Second, the address, "To the twelve tribes in the Dispersion," is elusive. What does this mean? Should one read the phrase literally, or might it have a symbolic significance? In the latter part of the chapter we will examine this phrase, and how it has been interpreted by recent scholars of James. Then in chapter four we will address the social and theological questions and problems with which the author and audience may be grappling when we examine what scholars are saying about the major themes and issues in James.

James the Just

The opening verse of the letter identifies "James a slave of God and of the Lord Jesus Christ" as the author of the letter. There are no details as to when or where this person was writing, no specific coworkers mentioned, and apart from identifying himself as a teacher in 3:1, no autobiographical information as in the undisputed letters of Paul. The author does not claim to be an apostle, which probably excludes some other figure named James in the New Testament, such as James the son of Zebedee (e.g., Mark 1:19), who becomes a follower of Jesus, and James, the son of Alphaeus, who is included as one of the twelve disciples (Mark 3:18). Moreover, based upon the extant evidence, these figures named James do not become as significant in the early church as James the Just, also known as James the brother of Jesus and James of Jerusalem.

Most contemporary scholars, whether they think that the letter was actually written by someone named James or not, concur that the text claims to be by this particular James, the James of Jerusalem. Admittedly, the evidence for such a conclusion is not profuse. The argument generally made is that James the Just is the best-known James of the early church, and thus a letter that simply claims to be by James, a "slave" or "servant" of Jesus Christ, with no other qualification, indicates an assumption that people would know who this James is. The Letter of Jude supposes that there was a well-known James with its opening verse: "Jude, a servant of Jesus Christ and brother of James" (Jude 1). Several other New Testament texts point to the significance of this figure, such as Paul, who refers to "James, the Brother of the Lord" (Gal 1:19), whom he met in Jerusalem, and whom the apostle also refers to as one of the "pillars" along with Cephas and John (Gal 2:9). James is mentioned in 1 Corinthians 15:7 as one of the people to whom the risen Christ appeared, although here Paul may be citing what is understood to be a pre-Pauline tradition—a body of material that existed within the Christian tradition that Paul incorporated into his letter to the Corinthians.[1] James gives a mediating speech in Acts 15:13–21 and, according to Acts 21:17–18, Paul visits James in Jerusalem. This James again appears in the Gospel of Mark when Jesus is teaching in the synagogue. Some astonished onlookers ask if this is indeed "the carpenter, the son of Mary, the brother of James and Joses…?" (Mark 6:3). The same story appears in Matthew (Matt 13:53–58) and Luke (Luke 4:16–30), although both of the latter gospels have quite different wordings, especially Luke, which does not refer to Mary or to Jesus' siblings, only to Jesus as Joseph's son. In his recent book on James of Jerusalem, Patrick Hartin has worked through each of these gospel passages and addressed the question of how one is to understand references to people as "brothers" or "sisters" of Jesus, as there have been different responses to this question within the Christian tradition.[2]

In addition, this James receives attention outside the New Testament in the writings of the first-century Jewish historian Josephus, who describes how James, the brother of Jesus, is delivered up by the High Priest in Jerusalem, Ananus, to be stoned for transgressing the Law in 62 CE.[3] Josephus tells us that fair-minded and law-observant inhabitants of Jerusalem are offended by this execution and as a result, Ananus is removed from his position. This account indicates that Josephus certainly thought that there was a historical person named James, who was the brother of Jesus, and who was well respected in Jerusalem circles. The early church historian, Eusebius of Caesarea, who lived from approximately 260 to 339 CE, also describes the death of James, relying upon three earlier sources: Josephus; Hegesippus, a late second-century Christian writer; and Clement of Alexandria, who lived during the early third century CE. Eusebius quotes the section of Josephus that was just discussed but also includes another quotation that may not be original to Josephus because it is not found in his extant writings. The quotation links the siege of Jerusalem by the Romans to the actions of revolutionary Jews who wanted to avenge the death of James the Just, who was known to be very righteous.[4] Eusebius's use of Hegesippus is more extensive. Hegesippus apparently recounted the death of James, whom Hegesippus refers to as "the Just" and describes this death as one of a righteous Jewish Christian martyr.[5] Finally, the references to Clement of Alexandria are very interesting, for Clement apparently narrates how James is chosen to be bishop of Jerusalem by some of the apostles, and how James, John and Peter receive the tradition from Jesus and pass it on to the apostles and then to the seventy. Regardless of whether or not such things took place, Clement clearly thinks that James is an important person.[6]

Various second-century writings also attest to the importance of James. Among these, the *Gospel of the Hebrews*, preserved only in fragments in other literature, presents James as the first witness to the resurrection of Jesus.[7] Some of the writings attributed to Clement of Rome also stress the importance of James as a pious Jewish Christian and James is again identified as a "bishop" of the church in Jerusalem.[8] The *Gospel of Thomas*, one of a collection of texts found in the mid-twentieth century at Nag Hammadi in Egypt, contains a fascinating verse in which the disciples ask Jesus who should be their leader once Jesus has departed, and he tells them to go to James the Righteous.[9] Other writings found in this collection include the *Apocryphon of James* as well as the *First and Second Apocalypses of James*. In all three texts James is portrayed as the recipient of special revelations from Jesus, which James then hands on to others. Finally, there is the *Protoevangelium of James*, which focuses upon the birth of Mary, the mother of Jesus. This text also wishes to assert the perpetual virginity of Mary, and thus it presents James as a stepbrother of Jesus. It states that Joseph was old when he came to marry Mary, and that he already had sons.[10] Although one of these sons is not directly identified as James, the author, who has witnessed the birth of Jesus, identifies himself as James,[11] and the text is ascribed to Jesus' "brother" James.[12] Thus it is clear that the figure of James of Jerusalem was important to a variety of forms of early Christianity as witnessed by this array of extant writings.

In particular, James was significant within a form of Christianity often referred to as "Jewish Christianity." This term is difficult because both first-century Judaism and first-century Christianity were diverse, and thus determining what is Jewish and what is Christian in these formative years is not obvious. Some scholars today prefer to refer to "ancient Judaisms" and "ancient Christianities" and a consultation at the Society of Biblical Literature as well as a collection of essays on the topic of Jewish Christianity attempts to address the term "Jewish Christianity" anew.[13] Study of the figure of James has been a means for examining this topic of Jewish Christianity, and a variety of recent books, including the work of John Painter, Pierre Antoine Bernheim and two significant collections of essays, one edited by Bruce Chilton and Craig Evans, and the other by Bruce Chilton and Jacob Neusner,[14] have centered on James, and from this focus, opened up a variety of areas for the discussion of Jewish Christianity. Until recently, this area of Christian origins has been largely neglected, as has the figure of James the Just. As Finnish scholar Matti Myllykoski's survey article on the figure of James the Just in contemporary scholarship points out, this neglect has "deep roots in Protestant scholarship, which treated it as a socially marginal and theologically inferior phenomenon in the history of early Christianity."[15] Fortunately, this trend has changed, and now scholars of all backgrounds study Jewish Christianity and the figure of James, as well as the letter that bears his name.

James and the Early Church

One more issue pertinent to current debates about the authorship of James needs to be addressed briefly: namely the reception of the Letter of James by the early Christian church. In particular, this requires attention to the formation of the New Testament canon, or official list of texts that were deemed authoritative for Christianity. This canon was not secure in the first centuries of Christianity, and there were debates about what should be included and why or why not. In 367 CE, Athanasius (c. 296–373 CE), a bishop in Alexandria who eventually went to Rome, is the first to list the twenty-seven books that exist today in the New Testament as canonical, although it took approximately two hundred more years before the canon became consistent among Christian groups.

Prior to Athanasius, the first Christian that we know of to cite the Letter of James as scripture is Origen of Alexandria (185–254 CE), who identifies the author as James.[16] Thus we know that some Christians in Egypt knew of the letter in the late second century. There are no extant references to the text in Alexandria prior to Origen, however.[17] Considering the popularity and authority of the figure of James, as witnessed by the number of texts that either talk about his death, identify him as a bishop or claim his name as the author of a specific writing, it is odd that if a letter bearing his name was in circulation, it is not cited prior to Origen. Eusebius of Caesarea points out that James, Jude, 2 Peter and the second and third epistles of John are "disputed books" in his *Ecclesiastical History*,[18] although Eusebius, an admirer of Origen, includes James as canonical.[19]

In the western church of Rome, we have no explicit evidence that James was included in the canon prior to the fourth century, when it shows up in the writings of Hilary of Poitiers sometime between 356 and 360 CE.[20] James is noticeably absent from the Muratorian Canon, a list of texts generally understood to be canonical for the Roman church and often dated to approximately 200 CE. A variety of authors have argued that James was known and used by earlier works produced or known in Rome such as *1 Clement* and the *Shepherd of Hermas*, but these arguments are based upon linguistic and thematic parallels with James; there are no specific citations from the letter nor attributions of the language and themes to the letter's author. Indeed, commentator Sophie Laws's argument that James finds its provenance in Rome is built in part on her conviction that the second-century CE *Shepherd of Hermas* knew and used ideas and phrases from the letter.[21] Luke Timothy Johnson also thinks that James was known by the *Shepherd*, yet he does not conclude that James was written in Rome, as we shall see.[22]

The precise manner in which James came to be included in the New Testament canon is a thorny issue. Some, such as Johnson, have argued that the influence of Rufinus (345–410 CE), St. Jerome (342–420 CE) and St. Augustine (354–430 CE), all admirers of Origen, was instrumental in the inclusion of James, although as we have seen, Johnson thinks that the letter was already known in the west.[23] Recently, however, Jonathan Yates has argued that Athanasius introduced James to the church at Rome. Although Athanasius's list of canonical texts does not appear until 367 CE, it does not reflect his thinking about the canon only in that year, as Yates points out. Athanasius was likely shaping his thoughts on the canon at least twenty if not thirty years prior to 367 CE, which also explains why the reference to James in Hilary of Poitiers appears before 367 CE.[24]

The history of the formation of the New Testament canon in the first few centuries of the Common Era is very difficult as the evidence is somewhat haphazard, and some sources are only available because they have been embedded, in part, within later sources. Overall, James's entry into the canon is late compared to other New Testament texts. This is especially true for the western church, where it does not appear explicitly until the fourth century. Some suggest, however, that James was already known in the west, even by second-century texts such as *Hermas*. Others think that James was accepted in the west because of Alexandrian influence, whether it is that of Athanasius, or of admirers of Origen such as Augustine and Jerome. Moreover, the fact that James is not explicitly cited until Origen despite the traditions about and texts attributed to James of Jerusalem in the second century is evidence for some that the letter is relatively late, because if early, one would expect to see it quoted. These points are relevant for some authors who try to determine the authorship and date of James.

The Author

For centuries, many assumed that James the Just was the author of this text. However, there were always those who questioned this "traditional" view, including Martin Luther, who famously labeled James a "right strawy epistle," and stuck it in the appendix of his German translation of the New Testament, with no page numbers.[25] Many others also argued that James was pseudonymous (literally, "false author"), which means that although the letter claims to be by someone named James, the real author used this name to give authority and legitimacy to the letter, as James of Jerusalem clearly was an important figure in the early church. Writing pseudonymously was common in antiquity, and sometimes the motivation for claiming a famous name was to honor the figure in whose name one wrote. This is not to say that writing pseudonymously was endorsed in the ancient world, just as it is not now. One of the reasons James came to be part of the Christian canon was because those who supported its inclusion *thought* that the letter was written by James of Jerusalem, whether or not it truly was.

Pseudonymous Authorship

There is a range of reasons why many contemporary scholars question the traditional view of authorship. These arguments are not all new, but have lingered as objections to the traditional view for some time. For example, Martin Dibelius and, more recently, Sophie Laws, point out that the figure of James of Jerusalem, as we can reconstruct him from the various sources delineated above, does not match the letter. If the author was the brother or close relative of Jesus, why does he not refer to him more ("Jesus Christ" appears in 1:1 and 2:1)? Moreover, James of Jerusalem was known to be a righteous Jew, concerned about the Law, including ritual matters (see Gal 2:12),[26] yet according to Dibelius and Laws the letter focuses upon the Law in a moral sense, without reference to ritual concerns (see Jas 1:27; 2:10).[27] For Laws, this raises the question of whether the author was a Jewish Christian at all, and indeed, in her 1992 *Anchor Bible Dictionary* article on James, she postulates that the author is a "God-fearer" or a Gentile who was attracted to "Jewish philosophy, but who did not fully convert to Judaism."[28]

Laws provides another reason for rejecting James as the author: namely the style and language of the letter. Clearly, James was written by someone who had a mastery of the Greek language as evident in its use of rare vocabulary and literary and stylistic techniques already discussed in the previous chapter. It also draws upon traditions from the Septuagint (the Greek translation of the Hebrew Scriptures that includes some other texts often referred to as the Deuterocanonical books, abbreviated LXX). One wonders how a relative of a Galilean artisan, whose first language was most likely Aramaic, could have produced such a text.[29] And as mentioned earlier, Laws thinks that there is a connection between James and the *Shepherd of Hermas*, which indicates a likely provenance of Rome for the letter.

According to Wiard Popkes, the issue of the letter's relationship to Pauline teaching is the most convincing reason for assigning James pseudonymous authorship and an approximate date of the turn of the first century.[30] For Popkes, James is written to confront a community that has been exposed to Paul's teaching about faith, works, and freedom, found especially in Galatians and Romans, but which has perverted this teaching, or simply allowed it to deteriorate, so that it has become empty of meaning and action. He understands the addressees' position to be that justification by faith comes easily, and thus they have become too open to the world and lax in their responsibilities to help others.[31] Thus the points of contact that Popkes sees between James 2:14–26 and a form of Paulinism are crucial for his sense of when to date the letter, and obviously, his firm rejection of traditional authorship.

Wesley Hiram Wachob thinks that James is an early text but does not assign to it "traditional" authorship. Wachob does not dwell on purported points of contact between James and Paul, admits that "it is possible" that the author of James knew of views similar to those of Paul, and even that he opposed such views. However, says Wachob, James's description of the Law draws upon "conventional values...[that] resonate with the 'text of culture' from which his epistle emanates."[32] For Wachob, the letter is directed to Jewish Christians in the dispersion, and wishes to be heard as James, the brother of Jesus. Wachob's comparison of James 2:5 with QMatt 5:3[33] leads him to argue that the implied author "is made to speak the same wisdom that Jesus spoke."[34] Indeed, the connection that Wachob sees between James and a pre-Matthean Sermon on the Mount is evidence that James is indeed an early text, written before the fall of Jerusalem in 70 CE, which shows no dependence upon the written gospels, the earliest of which (Mark) is usually dated around 70 CE. [35]

Todd Penner argues that the letter is early as well. He rejects the notion that James cannot be from first-century Palestine based upon its polished Greek because of the degree of Hellenism that had penetrated the region. Although the ostensible conflict between James 2:14–26 and Paul's ideas (or a distortion of Paul's ideas) about faith and works found in Galatians and Romans is a key reason for a relatively late dating of James, Penner claims that there is no conclusive evidence for connections between James and Paul. Penner points out that James appears to be completely unfamiliar with large parts of Galatians and Romans, and that in fact, James makes less sense as a response to Paul's teaching, than as drawing from a common tradition in which the connections between faith, works and righteousness were already established.[36] Although he does not claim that James of Jerusalem is the author, Penner thinks that the letter is early, and contains a teaching that is not from a marginal sector of early Christianity, but "possibly represents the heart and soul of the ministry of Jesus as a reformist prophet within Judaism."[37]

Scholarship has recently discussed the date of James in light of the formation of the New Testament canon. Robert W. Wall has examined the letter in light of the development of a collection of the seven letters known as the Catholic Epistles (James, 1 and 2 Peter, 1, 2, and 3 John and Jude), which in turn, became part of the New Testament. According to Wall, this collection probably took shape in the fourth century, and with its inclusion of James as a frontispiece, could effectively operate within the canon as a "functional Pauline criticism."[38] Wall demonstrates how James, as the first letter in the Catholic Epistle collection, introduces several theological themes that unify the letters.[39] The Catholic Epistle collection, appearing in the canon after the Acts narrative with its particular depiction of some of the key figures in the early church, including James of Jerusalem, would function as a balance to the Pauline letter collection. For Wall,

> the reception of Jas cues the church's critical concern about a reductionistic use of Pauline tradition that edits out the church's Jewish legacy, especially an ethos that resists any attempt to divorce a profession of orthodox beliefs from an active obedience to God's law in a pattern of salvation.[40]

Wall does not directly address the issue of the authorship of James, but David Nienhaus builds from Wall's work in his argument for pseudonymity. Nienhaus states, like Wall, that James forms a "bridge-text" to the other Catholic Epistles through linkages he sees between them. For Nienhaus, James was actually composed for this purpose, so that the Catholic Epistle collection could counterbalance the Pauline letter collection.[41] Thus James is probably a second-century pseudepigraph written in opposition to groups that had taken Pauline teachings to such an extreme that they were being used to support anti-Jewish and antinomian teachings. Nienhaus therefore concurs with those scholars who think that the author of James is familiar with Pauline thought, but also says that James is in contact with a collection of Pauline letters and engages them in order to correct a particular misunderstanding of Paul's thought that some Christians of the day are attempting to spread.[42]

Authentic Authorship

Obviously, for those who support the "traditional" authorship of James, there is much more of a consensus about the relative date of the letter, for it must have been written before 62 CE, when James of Jerusalem was killed. For some, the letter thus becomes the earliest text of the New Testament, while for others it still may postdate some of Paul's writings, and thus could have emerged from the late 50s up until the death of James. It is also important to indicate here that most scholars viewed James as a pseudepigraph for many decades in the modern era. However, a significant amount of recent scholarship on James has reasserted that James of Jerusalem is the author. Although none of these scholars can prove that this figure wrote the text, they do not see sufficient evidence to render his authorship impossible.

James B. Adamson, for example, argues that James of Jerusalem is the best candidate for authorship. One of the most conclusive pieces of evidence, he says, is that the speech of James in Acts 15:13–21 and the subsequent letter embedded in Acts 15:23–29, which Adamson thinks is by James, cohere with the letter of James. Adamson points to stylistic features that he sees shared by these texts, especially the use of the word *anaskeua-zontes* ("unsettling"—see Acts 15:24), which he understands to be reflective of the "vivid and resourceful vigor of the style of the Epistle of James."[43] He also examines the content of the letter, finding that it reflects a "pre-christological, almost pre-crucifixion stage" of early Christianity, is full of the sayings of Jesus expressed in James's own way and shows no trace of "disappointment over a delayed parousia."[44] Finally, Adamson does not see a conflict between James and Paul; rather the Letter of James is pre-Pauline, and is simply not influenced by Paul's ideas, be they on justification, faith, works or the death and resurrection. In sum, Adamson thinks that the letter was written by James of Jerusalem, perhaps in the early 40s CE, thereby making it the earliest text in the New Testament.

Douglas J. Moo also argues for authenticity based, in part, on similarities between the speech and letter in Acts 15 and the Letter of James. He thinks that the letter reflects the circumstances of the date and setting in which James of Jerusalem was living.

Specifically, he connects the condemnation of wealthy landown-
ers in James 5:1–6 to the plight of first-century Palestinian Jewish
Christians who have been forced to leave their homes in Palestine
and are now facing persecution from the rich. Moreover, Moo
thinks that what he terms the "primitive Christian theology" of
the letter, which he deems to "rarely go beyond accepted OT and
Jewish perspectives," could be associated with James the brother
of Jesus.[45] Moo also engages the objections to traditional authorship such as the argument that a Greek letter of such literary qual-
ity could not be produced by a first-century Palestinian Jew. Moo
rejects this argument using the findings of Martin Hengel, who
has documented the degree to which Hellenism had disseminated
through Palestine by the first century.[46] Moo addresses and
attempts to refute other challenges, such as the letter's attitude
towards Jewish Law, which as others have pointed out, does not
cohere with the presentation of James of Jerusalem's perspective,
the lack of reference to the close relationship between James and
Jesus, and the possibility of James 2 engaging with Pauline
thought. Moo thinks that James was not necessarily familiar with
an accurate version of Paul's teachings, and posits an early date of
James in the middle 40s of the first century.[47]

Another defender of traditional authorship, Luke Timothy
Johnson, engages some of the objections that Moo does, such as
the language of the letter and the possibility of interaction with
Pauline thought. Regarding the latter, Johnson argues that close
examination of James 2:14–26 and Pauline teaching on justification by faith reveals that the two authors are dealing with separate
issues, and that "it is because both Paul and James derive their
symbols from a Palestinian Jewish milieu that their language and
examples converge."[48] It is notable that Johnson does not think
that a comparison between the letter of James and the passages
from Acts 15 that Adamson and Moo address is an argument for
authenticity, for as Johnson says, the similarities here are easily
explained by both documents' common background in the language of the Septuagint (LXX).[49] However, Johnson then develops

a list of reasons why he thinks it possible that James of Jerusalem could have written the letter, although he grants that this can never be proven. Very briefly, these reasons are the following: the letter lacks the signs of late, pseudonymous authorship such as a clear attempt to prove the author's identity or authority and very little development of doctrine; the letter evidences the social conditions and lack of institutionalization characteristic of newer sects; the letter draws on some form of Jesus' teachings comparable to the sayings source Q;[50] the similarities and differences between James's and Paul's letters can be explained by both writers emerging from cultures indebted to Greco-Roman traditions but also defined by the symbolism and the narratives from the Torah; there are incidental details in James, such as the early and late rains (Jas 5:7) and others, that reflect Palestinian provenance; and finally, since Johnson thinks that *1 Clement*, which is often dated to the late first century, knew James, James must have been written "at a substantially earlier date."[51]

Richard Bauckham also joins the ranks of contemporary scholars who assert, or perhaps one should say *do not reject*, the authenticity of the letter. His argument is more a refutation of the reasons why scholars reject authenticity than it is a presentation of reasons why James should be understood as the author. He thinks that since the prescript of the letter presents an "epistolary situation" that is perfectly comprehensible within the context of James's leadership of the Jerusalem church, that "[t]he burden of proof... lies on those who contest its authenticity."[52] In addition, Bauckham rejects the notion that a first-century Jew from Palestine could not write a letter so permeated by Hellenistic ideas and style, although he does grant that James may have had some assistance from a native Greek-speaking scribe. Moreover, Bauckham counters the claim made by some that the implied author of the letter had a primarily moral notion of the Law that conflicts with the image of James as a person deeply concerned with ritual and dietary practices. For Bauckham, that the letter emphasizes the moral law is to be expected since the missive is directed, in his view, to Jewish Christians, and is not concerned with the question of Gentile converts at all.[53]

A few scholars have developed more of a compromise position although they still think that the letter is quite early; that is, pre-70 CE. Peter Davids thinks that the letter could have emerged in two stages whereby James the Just produced series of homilies, which were then crafted together into final form with the aid of a scribe more schooled in Greek style and rhetoric.[54] This view effectively enables one to posit authentic authorship and account for the elegant Greek. In his latest book on James of Jerusalem, Hartin presents the aforementioned view as a possibility, but shows preference for the idea that the letter was composed in the immediate aftermath of James of Jerusalem's death by a disciple of James, familiar with his teacher's thought, who writes in order to impart James's wisdom to those people who needed it. For Hartin, even if this scribe actually wrote the text, the voice of James of Jerusalem still lies behind it for "the writer clearly sees himself faithfully handing on the spirit of James's teaching for communities who acknowledged his [James's] authority."[55]

Conclusion

These are only a few examples of recent scholars who argue for pseudonymous, authentic or a combined authorship of James. Various reasons are provided for these positions, often hinging on issues related to the language and style of the letter, to what degree it may interact with Pauline teachings or letters, whether it reflects the characterization of James of Jerusalem found in the New Testament and other ancient texts, as well as issues related to the inclusion of the letter in the New Testament canon. Even though this question is sure to remain contested for some time, its exploration has contributed to the study of the figure of James of Jerusalem and indirectly, to the notion of "Jewish Christianity," a topic of research that has gained considerable momentum within the past few decades. Although we may not be able to solve the question of the authorship of the letter of James in the near future, the attempts to understand its origins provide opportunities to further examine the complexities of ancient Judaisms and Christianities.

The Audience

Disagreements about the audience of James also open windows to the complexities just mentioned. Unlike Paul's letters, the text of James does not identify specific communities to which it is directed, only the "twelve tribes in the Dispersion." How then, does one understand this phrase and what are the implications of this understanding for determining the identity of the intended audience?

A common view, upheld for example, by François Vouga, is that this phrase is to be understood as a metaphorical reference to "the true Israel."[56] Assuming that the audience is Christian, and given the references to Christians as "Israel" (Gal 6:16) and as living in the "Dispersion" (1 Pet 1:1) in other early Christian texts, scholars such as Vouga have argued that "the twelve tribes in the Dispersion" can be understood completely metaphorically as people living in spiritual exile. Some scholars such as Dibelius[57] and Matthias Konradt[58] think that these people are Gentiles, while others think that they are Jewish, or possibly a combination of both. David Hutchinson Edgar, who concurs that a metaphorical reading of "twelve tribes in the Diaspora" is most appropriate, thinks that the audience shares a Jewish worldview. He points out, however, that one should not assume clear boundaries between Christians and Jews when approaching literature from this period, nor should one understand the "Jewish Christian" recipients of James as distinct from "mainstream" Judaism.[59]

Other scholars emphasize the eschatological or "end time" dimension of "twelve tribes in the Dispersion." Based upon his analysis of the use of "twelve tribes" in ancient Jewish texts, Matt Jackson-McCabe argues that its presence at the beginning of

James "connotes the view that God's promise to Israel is at present unfulfilled."[60] Jackson-McCabe does not reject the possibility that the phrase could also refer to the geographical location of the intended audience, but he stresses the eschatological sense of the phrase, especially when it appears just after a reference to Jesus Christ. The rest of the letter coheres well with this view, with the promise that the poor will inherit the kingdom (Jas 2:5–7), the anticipated destruction of the rich in chapter 1 and chapter 5, and the opposition between God and the world. In a similar vein, Todd Penner interprets James 1:1 as possessing eschatological significance although he thinks that the reference to the twelve tribes in the Dispersion could also be understood in a spiritual sense in the manner that Dibelius and others have presented.[61]

Timothy Cargal has a unique approach to the phrase because he analyzes the letter, as noted in the previous chapter, through the lenses of structural semiotics. Although he adopts a metaphorical reading of "Dispersion," he interprets it in correspondence with the closing verses of the letter, which offer instruction for those who "wander from the truth" (Jas 5:19–20). Thus, being in the "Dispersion" is equivalent to being lost, or having strayed from the truth.[62] This is an intriguing approach to understanding the reference to "Dispersion" in James, although there is little historical evidence that ancient Jews or Christians would have used the term in this way.

In contrast to the metaphorical interpretations, some scholars understand "twelve tribes in the Dispersion" literally, as referring to Jewish Christians (although the letter never uses the word "Christian") living outside of Palestine. Patrick Hartin is a significant proponent of this view, observing that "the whole tone of this letter is one that shows knowledge of the world of Israel."[63] He thinks that James emerges "at a time when the separation between the traditions of the house of Israel and the traditions of Christianity had not occurred"[64] although the letter also falls in line with the trajectory of the Jesus tradition and maintains loyalty to Jesus' mission.[65] Thus James's vision "still lies at the heart of the world of Israel and sees no incompatibility between being a follower of Jesus and an adherent of Israel's traditions."[66] Hartin also thinks that the eschatological dimension of the reference is important to underline, for it is a reminder that the letter stands within the long tradition of Israel's hope for a "restoration" of the twelve-tribe kingdom.[67]

Recently Dale Allison has revived a third option for understanding this address. I say "revived" because as Allison points out, this possibility was held by many early commentators on James, but has been ignored in recent decades.[68] Allison argues that the letter is a pseudepigraph, addressed to both Jewish Christians and Jews who do not accept Christian convictions. Part of his argument rests on his suspicion that the reference to "Jesus Christ" in James 2:1 is not original to the letter, but a later addition. The other reference to Jesus Christ, in James 1:1, identifies the author as a member of the Jesus movement, but does not assume that the entire audience holds to Christian teaching. The purpose of the letter, argues Allison, is to function as a type of apology that offers both edification for the Jewish Christian adherents in the audience and clarification to those Jewish audience members who are not Christian.[69] Thus James reflects "a first-century Christian group still battling for its place within the Jewish community, a Christian group that wishes to remain faithful members of the synagogue, to be…both Jew and Christian."[70] The letter serves as a way of promoting tolerance for Jewish Christians in a place where there was possibly increasing antipathy towards them from other Jews.

Building upon Allison's work, John S. Kloppenborg also argues for this dual audience of both Diaspora or Dispersion Judeans and members of the Jesus movement.[71] He understands the address to the "twelve tribes in the Diaspora" literally; that is, to refer to Judeans outside of Palestine some of whom are members of the Jesus movement. Kloppenborg concurs with Allison that the reference to "Jesus Christ" in James 2:1 is an interpolation, and thinks that the absence of "overtly 'Christian' beliefs and formulae is deliberate" in order to create common ground between these two groups, as opposed to setting forth the distinct ideas emerging from the Jesus movement.[72] The letter is comparable to Jewish Diaspora letters in a variety of ways, but differs in that it does not hold out a return from the Diaspora as a promise or solution to the problems that the audience faces. Rather, James, like Philo, stresses control of the passions through obedience to Torah as a means of facing the threats of desire and "friendship with the world" (Jas 4:4).[73]

Conclusion

Contemporary scholars clearly have not come to an agreement regarding the authorship, date or audience of the letter. Although we did not focus on the provenance of the letter, there is no agreement on that issue either. Those who uphold a traditional or a "James with some scribal assistance" view of authorship usually place James within Palestine, while others, such as Laws, see the letter emerging from Rome. However, questions of from what geographic location the letter emerged remain open as Greek language and ideas had spread so thoroughly throughout the Mediterranean basin by the first century CE.

Despite the lack of agreement on these historical issues, continued analysis of James, with an eye to these questions, is important. Thinking about why James was written or why it was included in the Christian canon enables further reflection about the struggles and controversies of the early church. If James was written before Judaism and Christianity were noticeably separated from one another, the letter offers a glimpse of Jewish Christianity, or Christian Judaism, for which we have comparatively little information from the ancient world. Thus even if the mystery of the origins of James cannot be solved, at least not in the near future, its pursuit can lead to new insights as to what ancient religions shared in common, how they developed or how one particular religion took on a diversity of forms.

3
THEMATIC ISSUES IN JAMES

The Letter of James reflects a wide variety of concerns and topics, some of which have been subject to a long history of scholarship, such as the relationship between James and Paul on the question of faith and works, as well as newer foci of inquiry, including how James may be challenging the influence of wealthy patrons. This chapter will examine these developments in scholarship under separate thematic headings, but the reader should remain aware that many of these themes are interconnected. Moreover, space does not permit analysis of every issue in James, only those most widely discussed in recent decades. We will begin with an exploration of the ways in which James is understood in relation to Paul and his letters, for this topic remains contested, with a wide range of viewpoints.

James and Paul

It is well known that one of the factors responsible for the relative neglect of James for many years was that it was viewed negatively by Martin Luther. To Luther, James appeared to contradict the notion of justification by faith, a feature very important for Luther's theology,[1] and Luther relegated the text to the margins of the canon, along with some other texts, such as the Letter of

Jude, for which he had little sympathy. Although most Reformation theologians did not share Luther's antipathy for James, his judgment of the text undoubtedly contributed to the subordination of James to Paul within Protestant traditions.[2]

Today, however, with the rise of interest in James, some scholars prefer to read James without any reference to Paul, pointing out that that there may not be any relation whatsoever between the two, and that besides, James deserves to be read on its own terms.[3] In a recent commentary on James and Jude, for example, William F. Brosend II suggests that the two letters be read without any presumed relationship to the letters of Paul or Peter, which, for him, supports an early dating and authentic authorship. He thinks that James and Jude were written by the brothers of Jesus and that James need not be understood as a reaction to Paul's thought, as many other scholars have thought.[4] However, a variety of authors, as we shall see, continue to see a real conflict if not contradiction between James and Paul, or between James and a particular understanding of Paul's thought, while others understand them to have a harmonious relationship and still others perceive that James might be described as a "document of Paulinism."[5]

James and Pauline / Post-Pauline Communities at Odds

A dominant view within New Testament scholarship has been that James 2:14–26 is a critical response to Paul's emphasis upon justification by faith, and this view continues to prevail among some contemporary scholars albeit in different ways. Vasiliki Limberis, for example, understands James 2:17–26 as a direct response to Paul's teaching in Galatians 3. James, who for Limberis is the authentic James of Jerusalem, wrote his letter after Paul's Jerusalem visit, during which James "probably heard Paul's view on Abraham and faith in person when Paul arrived in Jerusalem in 56."[6] James objects to Paul's ideas because in James's view, Paul has stressed Abraham's faith and promise while "decoupling" Abraham from the Law, which in James's and other Jewish writers' opinion, Abraham upheld in its entirety, and which included "works" of mercy and hospitality.[7] For James, Paul is wrong because he has misinterpreted Abraham, and separated works and faith. James, writing within the Law-observant mission to the Gentiles, thus attempts to correct these faulty understandings and stress that Abraham kept the entire Law, which includes doing works of mercy and hospitality while remaining faithful to God. James 2 is squarely against Galatians 3.

R. Jason Coker also sees a direct conflict between James and Paul, although he thinks that this opposition is not so focused on the faith/works issue as it is on that of identity. Coker innovatively uses post-colonial criticism in his analysis of James's and Paul's letters, arguing that James demonstrates nativist resistance to colonial power, "which is characterized by reproducing colonial representations in order to resist colonial influence," while Paul's writings manifest hybrid resistance that blurs the boundaries between the colonizer and the colonized "in order to renegotiate a new set of power relations."[8] Paul is willing to advocate a mixed or hybrid identity that is neither purely native nor purely imperial. Various points in his letters support such a view, especially Galatians 2—3 and Romans 3—4, which reflect a faith/works binary using the example of Abraham, and effectively "blur[s] the boundaries between believers and non-believers, which James interprets as assimilation and compromise."[9] James 2:14–26 is a direct response to these ideas, which the author may not have read specifically in Galatians and Romans but heard from Paul at the Jerusalem council. In writing his letter, James both reminds his audience of Paul's ideas, then proceeds to refute them and stress a purely nativist identity that in its attempt to fight against the Roman empire, actually espouses the Roman imperial ideal of "pure native piety."[10] James possesses a deeply critical attitude towards the world and an emphasis upon works as central to religious identity, in contrast to Paul, who stresses faith as key and at some points allows for a certain accommodation to worldly and imperial practices. Ultimately, however, it was Paul's hybrid position that found a place in the Roman empire—an empire that eventually became Christian and "utterly forgot about the epistle of James."[11]

Other scholars do not understand James to be at odds with Paul's teaching itself but with the teachings and practices in Pauline communities post-Paul. For example, we already saw in the earlier chapter on authorship that Popkes thinks that the letter responds to particular developments in Pauline communities that had absorbed Paul's instruction on faith, works and freedom, but in which these teachings subsequently had been watered down, so that justification was perceived to be easy, leading communities to become too tolerant of worldly activities and derelict in their duties to assist others.[12] Likewise, Tsuji understands James as confronting developments in Pauline Christianity[13] and explores James's social teachings to show how his criticism of wealth fits within a larger critique of post-Pauline groups that have become too accommodating to worldly pursuits.

Kari Syreeni is another biblical scholar who contends that James is directed to Pauline communities, particularly the one in Corinth, after Paul's teachings had become established. Syreeni argues that the Letter of James is familiar with several of Paul's letters, including Romans, the Corinthian correspondence and possibly Galatians, and that it addresses a situation in Corinth where theological and social tensions had arisen between Jewish and Gentile Christians. Syreeni hypothesizes that James confronts a church in which the Jewish Christians and their Gentile sympathizers who had not broken off completely from the synagogue were enduring social and economic discrimination from new leadership. For Syreeni, these newer Gentile Christian leaders may be trying to develop liaisons with rich patrons, thus creating ties between the community and wider society which could threaten the Jewish minority. James thus stresses the superiority of the poor as well as an "ideological supremacy for the genuine Jewish legacy."[14] The letter writer disagrees with some aspects of what he understands to be Paul's teaching, particularly about aspects of the Law, but addresses a post-Pauline scenario. He deliberately draws upon some of Paul's ideas, however, in order to persuade the Gentile leadership to remain in solidarity with and to assist their Jewish brothers and sisters.

Harmony between James and Paul

In contrast to those who perceive a direct conflict with either the ideas of Paul himself or the developments within post-Pauline communities, some contemporary writers do not perceive significant tension between James and Paul, if any at all. In Luke Timothy Johnson's estimation, the focus on comparisons between sections of Galatians and Romans on righteousness and James 2:18–26 distorts the discussion, as in his view there are many points of similarity and dissimilarity between the two authors.[15] Overall, he thinks that Paul and James need not be understood as contesting each other's ideas but are each addressing their own sets of concerns. Despite the "remarkable points of resemblance" between portions of their respective letters,[16] Johnson argues that upon closer analysis, each author has a different focus. He works through several ideas in each text, pointing out, for example, that James has a different understanding of law, *nomos*, than Paul, and James does not link *nomos* to works, as Paul does. Johnson does not rule out a relationship between James and Paul, and indeed, since he thinks that the author of the letter is James of Jerusalem, he has to assume some sort of relationship, but he does not see the two writers at odds in the way that many other authors do.

Patrick Hartin, like Johnson, devotes a section of his commentary on James to exploring the relationship between James and Paul specifically on the topic of faith and works. Despite the shared vocabulary of "faith," "works," "Law," "justification" and "to save," James and Paul are not at odds but simply emphasize different aspects of these concepts.[17] Hartin works specifically through the notions of "justification" and "works," examining their meanings within the Hebrew Bible, early Christianity, Paul's letters and

James. He argues that Paul is focused on the situation of a person who has not come to faith, and who attempts to do so through works of the Law, which for Paul, do not justify. James, however, is concerned about the person who already has faith and stresses the importance of doing works in order to express that faith. Regarding works, like Johnson Hartin points out that when discussing justification, Paul refers to "works of the Law" and not James's more general "works" and that overall, Paul does expect the members of the church to do good works, as James does, and that the two are, in the end, on the same page when it comes to the question of doing good for others.

Thus Johnson and Hartin, while they do not absolutely dismiss some sort of relationship between James and Paul, downplay the differences, arguing that the two writers are really focusing on different dimensions of the terms and ideas that they share in common. Other contemporary authors, however, state that James's ideas in 2:14–26 have no connection with Paul, either positive or negative, but that the section is fully comprehensible in light of the context of first-century Judaisms. Donald Verseput argues that James 2:14–26 must be understood in light of James 1:26–27, which he understands to be consistent with the prophetic emphasis (see Isa 1:16–17) that cultic worship or "religion" that is pure and obedient (1:27) is one embodied by good works.[18] James 2:14–26 reflects this continued emphasis, indicating that works are not the product of faith, nor that faith is downgraded, but that faith, "one's godward service…cannot be divorced from righteous deeds, for obedience *is* the most holy form of faith."[19] Todd Penner thinks that James and Paul may both be relying upon an independent and well-established tradition that linked "faith," "works" and "righteousness" but that the two need not be dependent on each other and if anything, perhaps Paul is reading James and not vice versa.[20] The notion of criticizing those who do not manifest their faith through action is important within other New Testament texts (Matt 23:13–36) and thus James's ideas are quite at home in early Christian literature—it is Paul, in certain instances, who is the maverick.[21]

James and Paul within the Context of Canon Formation

Returning to the question of James and the canon, discussed briefly in the previous chapter, we see a few scholars today examining the relationship of James and Paul in light of the formation of the early Christian canon, especially the Pauline and Catholic letter collections. Nienhuis, building on the work of Wall, who has focused specifically on the development and theological coherence of the Catholic Epistle collection,[22] argues that James is a second-century document that, through deliberate intertextual links between both some the Catholic letters and a version of the Pauline letter collection, seeks to "create an apostolic letter collection based not on the dual authority of Peter and Paul, but on the ancient two-sided apostolic missions of Paul and the Jerusalem Pillars [see Gal 2:9]."[23] The pseudonymous author of James deliberately sought to bind his letter to those of Peter and John in order to develop a strong and literarily consistent message that presents itself as coming from the Jerusalem pillars. The Catholic letter collection would correct possible distortions of the Pauline message, specifically those associated with Marcionite emphases upon the rejection of the Torah and the continuity between Judaism and the Christian message. As Nienhuis states, texts such as 2 Peter and James came relatively late upon the scene, and reflect "these proto-catholic anti-Marcionite polemics in their content, primarily in their authorizing of the Jewish scriptures, and particular vision of apostolic harmony."[24] James thus does not function as an anti-Pauline text, but as one that seeks to correct the distortions of Paul that could arise when ancients sought to focus on the letters of Paul, to the exclusion of others.

Somewhat in the same vein, Margaret M. Mitchell has recently analyzed James in comparison to Paul's letters, arguing that the former served as a corrective to distortions of the latter.

Mitchell thinks that the author of James knew Galatians (and possibly Romans) and 1 Corinthians, and that he is writing from *within* Paulinism in order to produce a letter that will reconcile "'Paul with Paul' and 'Paul with the pillars.'"[25] The letter emerges from Gentile Christianity, knows and supports Paul's letters and draws upon them in order to reconcile seeming tensions among them (especially Gal 2:13 and 1 Cor 9:20–23 on "hypocrisy" and Gal 2:16 and 1 Cor 13:2 on "faith") as well as perceived conflicts between Paul and the Jerusalem leaders as evident in Galatians 2:11–14. James thus interprets Paul "toward the centre and away from extremes, and attempt[s] to show that the church had a concordant apostolic foundation."[26] Thus the letter is clearly not at odds with Paul's thought at all, but is purposefully written to promote harmony among Paul's letters and to promote the memory of Paul as someone in concord with the other apostles, notably the Jerusalem pillars.

We thus see that the relationship between James and Paul, or James and post-Pauline developments, is far from resolved. Some continue to argue the traditional view that the two are at odds, although not necessarily on the same grounds as earlier scholars did, whereas others see clear harmony between these texts. Clearly work needs to continue on this question.

Theological Issues

Although James does not provide sustained reflection on the significance of Jesus Christ, scholars today do not dismiss James as lacking in theological substance as they have in years past.[27] In the following section we will explore some of the theological topics that the letter engages. The indicator "theological" is a tricky one, because it is not clear that the author of James would somehow separate theological questions from social and moral ones, but for the sake of organization I will do so here, keeping in mind that they are always related, for James, to questions of how one lives in relation to others and to God.

Matthias Konradt has examined James with a focus on its theological dimensions, arguing, with others, that the letter is a coherent, systematic text. For Konradt, however, there is also a consistent theological concept throughout James, based primarily in James 1:18 with its reference to God's "word of truth."[28] James 1:18 is key not only to James 1:13–25 but to the letter as a whole; it indicates that the beginning of Christian existence is the receipt of the "word of truth" that is freely given by God. The rest of the letter then proceeds to describe dimensions of this Christian existence, which requires a continual hearing of and obedience to God's word. Such a life of obedience will culminate in salvation, which is again a gift of God. Other aspects of this Christian existence require distance from the sinful world, and true faith that must be based upon works without becoming a kind of works righteousness. Konradt's discussion, whether or not he is correct on all counts, shows that clearly James can be understood as a theologically consistent unity, and not at all a loose jumble of ideas, as many earlier interpreters have surmised.

Perfection

One of the themes that several theological approaches to James have centered upon is that of perfection, or completeness, a topic introduced in James 1:2–4. As we saw in the chapter on structure and rhetoric, Martin Klein understands perfection as a central theological emphasis of the letter, for perfection, especially moral perfection, is linked to the final judgment in which those who are ethically perfect will be saved.[29] Klein thus sees this notion of perfection in James as intrinsically linked to the eschatology of the letter. Hartin also focuses upon perfection as a central idea in James. Using comparative contextual materials, he argues that perfection refers to completeness or wholeness; that it requires the unconditional giving of oneself to God; and that it demands obedience to God's will and to the Torah or laws of God.[30] This perfection is a unifying theme in the letter that gives meaning to other issues that James develops such as testing, wisdom, the Law and works.[31] Like Klein, Hartin also understands perfection to have an eschatological characteristic insofar as at the coming judgment the audience "is to be found perfect and mature."[32]

Apocalyptic, Eschatology and Wisdom

By the first century, apocalyptic traditions were well developed within Judaism, and had a strong impact upon the development and creation of many early Christian texts. "Apocalyptic" refers to an "unveiling" or "revealing" of events, images, journeys, etc., that are revealed to an individual or community, and can take on many forms. Probably the most "apocalyptic" book in the New Testament is that of the Revelation of John. Apocalyptic often overlaps with a discussion of "eschatology," which is the study of the "last things," because apocalyptic events are associated with this moment in time when God will intervene and transform the world to a new reality. Such a combination of a revelation associated with the end times is often referred to as "apocalyptic eschatology," although ideas about eschatology developed earlier in the history of Israelite religion than those of apocalyptic did.

Wesley Hiram Wachob examines the role of apocalyptic as an important "intertexture" of the Letter of James. By "intertexture" he means the way in which James draws upon other traditions, both written and oral. Although the Letter of James is by no means an "apocalypse," for it does not contain visions, angels and seers typical of ancient Jewish and Christian apocalypses, it does address topics that "are typically associated with apocalyptic literature."[33] These topics include the *parousia* or coming of the Lord; judgment; justice; trials of faith; rich and poor; and the kingdom of God, and together, for Wachob, they support James's argument that the audience should live in the world with the same faith and obedience that Jesus possessed. Although James stresses how one should live in the present, the nearness of the end times informs the overall rhetoric of the letter.[34]

Another author who focuses upon the eschatological features of the letter is Todd Penner. In his book, Penner argues that James is a mixture of wisdom, or sapiential, and eschatological ideas but that the opening (Jas 1:2–12) and closing (Jas 4:6—5:12) of the letter form an *inclusio* that embodies an eschatological framework for the text as a whole.[35] In this sense, the rest of the letter manifests teachings for a community that understands itself to be nearing the final judgment. The combination of wisdom and eschatological teachings in James is not unique to the letter when one compares it to other ancient Jewish and Christian literature, and certainly the body of the letter focuses very much on the importance of receiving wisdom from God (see Jas 3:13–18). For Penner, however, this wisdom instruction is framed by references to the end times and thus this "eschatological focus of the framework pushes the community instruction in a particular direction: the community instruction is for the people living in the 'last days,' awaiting the imminent return of the Judge...."[36]

Although some have argued in the past that James is an example of wisdom literature,[37] the presence of these apocalyptic and eschatological themes indicates that it is not solely a wisdom text, but contains multiple categories of writing. James certainly draws upon topics found in Jewish wisdom literature, such as testing (Jas 1:2–4, 12–14; cf. Sir 2:1) and the tongue (see Sir 5:13–14), cites directly from wisdom texts such as Proverbs 3:34 in James 4:6, and as we have seen, treats wisdom as a theme in its own right (Jas 1:5; 3:13–18). Thus wisdom, as Peter H. Davids points out, "plays a decisive role" in James.[38] Davids even argues that there is a wisdom pneumatology (study of the spirit) in James; that "wisdom functions for James as the Spirit does for Paul,"[39] but others, such as Andrew Chester and Ralph P. Martin, do not find sufficient evidence for this claim, especially because James never mentions the "spirit" at all.[40] But in addition to wisdom, the letter also clearly contains eschatological and apocalyptic elements and therefore scholars such as Jackson-McCabe examine James not as a single genre but as a mixture of both wisdom and apocalyptic, noting with others that the overall motivation for the letter is the coming judgment.[41]

Similarly Hartin scrutinizes James with an eye to the genres of writing within it and concludes that James contains wisdom, prophetic, apocalyptic and eschatological traditions, thereby making it a "hybrid"[42] comparable to other texts such as the sayings source Q. Hartin was also one of the first to highlight the degree to which James shares particular features with a Jewish writing known as the *Epistle of Enoch* (1 Enoch 92–105) such as the fact that they are both addresses by a "patriarch" (James, Enoch) to spiritual descendants; they each contrast the righteous with the sinful and the respective fates that await them; and they both use similar literary forms such as woes and exhortations.[43] Hartin sees significant differences between the two texts, however, in the fact that although James makes it clear that the sinful are doomed to destruction (Jas 1:9–11; 5:1–6), the author does not provide detailed descriptions of what this destruction entails. Even though the promise of future judgment may serve to motivate life in the present, there is no revelation of a future world of God as there is the *Epistle of Enoch*. The *Epistle of Enoch*, in contrast, does include more extensive scenarios of what awaits both the unrighteous and the righteous in order to provide comfort to those who are suffering now. For Hartin, this important difference prevents him from classifying James as an "apocalypse" but, as stated earlier, as a combination of different types of literature.

Christology

Although, like Q, James does not reflect upon the significance of the death and resurrection of Jesus, some scholars have attempted to get at what sort of Christology, or understanding of the significance of Jesus Christ, James may reflect. Matt Jackson-McCabe, for example, examines the "mythic world" of James in light of Jewish messianic literature of the early Roman period, and concludes that it is quite possible that the "Judge" in James 5:9 could be a reference to Jesus.[44] According to Jackson-McCabe, James understands Jesus the Messiah, or Christ, in a manner comparable to other Jewish texts of the period, in which the Messiah will return, destroy the enemies of God and God's people and restore the twelve-tribe kingdom of Israel. Salvation is thus not tied to the death and resurrection, as it is for other early Christian writers (although for McCabe, James presupposes the death and resurrection) but to national restoration that will arrive soon, provided God's people continue to observe the Law, which the letter urges them to uphold in a variety of ways.[45]

Jackson-McCabe's study is an interesting approach to the Christology of the letter, for given that there are only two references to "Jesus Christ" in James (Jas 1:1; 2:1) and that some authors, as we have seen in an earlier chapter, consider the James 2:1 reference to be a later scribal addition, it is very difficult to tackle the Christology of James. The word *lord* (*kyrios*) refers at times to God (see Jas 3:9), but it is possible at other moments that it is a reference to Jesus (see Jas 5:7). Thus some scholars say that to try to find a "developed or explicit Christology is little more than special pleading."[46] Certainly James does not share a focus on the Holy Spirit, new creation or rebirth, as other prominent early Christian texts, such as the Gospel of John or the letters of Paul do, but it is possible that it represents a different way of understanding the significance of the Christ. And although it may presume the death and resurrection of Jesus, it does not, like the sayings source Q, indicate that such events are central to the salvation of the community. James does, however, bear many "echoes" of Jesus' teachings, and we will explore this issue in the following chapter.

The Law

It is clear that Jewish law—the Torah—is important for James; there is no criticism of the Law and in fact, it is taken for granted as something that the audience must uphold in full. As Chester and Martin point out, for James, as for Judaism generally, "the law is a joy and delight, not a burden."[47]

More specifically, James cites from the Law directly, quoting the love command from Leviticus 19:18 (LXX) in James 2:8. Luke Timothy Johnson has examined the use of Leviticus in James in detail, and argued that James not only refers to Leviticus 19 in 2:8, but that it is "virtually certain" that James 5:4 combines an allusion to Isaiah 5:9 (LXX) with one to Leviticus 19:13[48] given the use of Leviticus 19 elsewhere in the letter and based on examination of how another first-century Jewish text, *The Sentences of Pseudo-Phocylides*, uses the same chapter from Leviticus. In addition, Johnson goes on to say that there may in fact be four if not six more possible allusions to different parts of Leviticus 19:12–18 throughout James.[49] Based upon his analysis of the use of these allusions throughout the letter, Johnson concludes that for James, "keeping the law of love involves observing the *commandments* explicated by the Decalogue (2:11) and Leviticus 19:12–18 in their entirety."[50] Johnson does not discuss to what extent the cultic laws, such as food laws or circumcision, are important—indeed the letter is silent on these issues—but certainly the ethical commands of Judaism are upheld in James with great vigor.

Another recent study of the Law in James is Jackson-McCabe's book, which analyzes the notion of law as "logos" in Stoic writings. Jackson-McCabe argues that "the implanted word (logos)" of James 1:21 is referring to the Law, the Torah, as a written form of the divine law that Stoics associated with human reason. Other contemporary Jewish writers, such as Philo of Alexandria, adapted these Stoic ideas to their conceptions of the Law. Moreover, this law is connected to the notion of the "law of freedom" in James 1:25, and the "word [logos] of truth" in James 1:21. Likewise James has taken a Stoic tradition and associated it with the Torah—something that the Stoic writers obviously did not do. For Jackson-McCabe, James combines Jewish, Christian and Greek traditions to develop a letter in which "it is assumed that the Torah represents a written expression of the implanted *logos* that all human beings possess by nature; and it is expected that the god who authored this law will execute an eschatological judgment in accord with it at the *parousia* of Jesus Christ."[51]

Purity

We indicated above that James does not address particular cultic laws such as what to eat or circumcision, issues that were of considerable debate within some of the churches that Paul founded. Perhaps the letter writer simply assumed them? However, some contemporary authors have observed to what extent James addresses purity concerns. John H. Elliott's article applies the anthropologist Mary Douglas's concepts of purity and pollution to James as a whole. According to Douglas, these two concepts organize things into clean and unclean, whole and incomplete, within societies and could aid in supporting or substituting for moral guidelines.[52] Elliott sees these two concepts operating in James at the personal, social and cosmic levels. To be pure or holy is to have integrity (or perfection, as other scholars have discussed) such that faith and action cohere together, to live in solidarity with the community and to be loyal and committed to God. This is what it means to live with the wisdom from above. In contrast, to be impure involves doubting, falling prey to desire, not manifesting faith through works, not caring for others and being friends with the devil as opposed to being friends with God. This is what it means to live with the wisdom from below.[53] Elliott, as we have already seen, sees these three dimensions of the purity/pollution contrast functioning rhetorically to provide conceptual coherence to the letter as well, and joins other studies who understand integrity, perfection or wholeness as a focal theme in the text as a whole.

Darian Lockett also thinks that purity and pollution are important conceptual categories for understanding the letter of James, but he differs from Elliott in that he does not conflate purity with the notion of perfection. This is not to say that purity is wholly unrelated to perfection or wholeness, which he understands as major theme of the letter, but that it functions, with the contrasting notion of pollution, as a means of developing boundaries within the worldview of the letter.[54] Purity functions in particular as a necessary prerequisite for becoming perfect. Within the overall perspective of James, "the world" is associated with pollution ("stain" in Jas 1:27; 3:6) while pure piety is associated with God and includes caring for others (Jas 1:27). Moreover "the world" and all of its pollution and impiety is a symbol of an entire worldview that James presents to his audience, albeit one that he wants his readers to resist in favor of a worldview that requires purity and loyalty to God. This is not to say that James promotes some type of sectarian separation from society, but that he wants his readers to avoid some of the "alien values" of the world, such as patron-client relations and bad speech, which we will discuss presently. For Lockett then, James warns that "friendship with the world" (Jas 4:4), or the alignment of oneself with the values and activities of the world, is to be avoided. In order to emphasize this attitude, James draws upon purity and pollution language to develop clear boundaries and advocate a piety that is "pure and undefiled before God" (Jas 1:27).[55]

Anthropology

How does James understand human beings? Such a question is not easily answered through reading the letter, although given the author's pessimism about the tongue, as we shall see, it appears likely that he would not be too optimistic about human nature either. James is unusual, moreover, in explicitly stating that God does not tempt people but that "one is tempted by one's own desire, being lured and enticed by it" (Jas 1:14), yet he also, as we have seen, stresses human wholeness or perfection. Joel Marcus, who examines James 1:13b–14 in light of the concept of "inclination" or "intentionality," found in the Hebrew Bible, intertestamental texts such as Sirach, Qumran, Philo of Alexandria, the Testaments of the

Twelve Patriarchs and Rabbinic literature, equates the "desire" of James 1:14–15 with the notion of this "inclination" found in this background literature. Although this inclination can be positive or negative in comparative materials, he deduces that the idea of an "evil inclination" forms part of the anthropology of James, so that the one who overcomes this inclination through testing and suffering and perseverance is the one who is able to receive wisdom, follow the Law and not become prone to becoming double-minded and stained by the world.[56] Temptation, in James, is not from God (see Jas 1:13), but emerges from the "evil inclination, which is man's [sic] *own* inclination (1:13–14)."[57] This inclination has been placed in humans by God and can cause envy (see Jas 4:5), but God grants the human the grace to conquer it and thus "defeat the devil (4:6–7)."[58] Marcus notes that there are two *specific* references to the evil inclination in James—James 1:14–15 and James 4:5—but no clear references to a good inclination. Perhaps this is because James is not willing to ascribe an inherent goodness to humans, goodness emerging only from God.

More recently, Walter T. Wilson, who has also examined the anthropology of James, concurs that this "desire" in James conforms to the ancient understanding of "inclination" discussed by Marcus and others.[59] Wilson develops this dimension of the letter, showing how this evil inclination in James is gendered, for "desire" is personified as a woman who lures and entices the human, then conceives and gives birth to sin, which when grown, brings forth death (see Jas 1:14–15). This aspect of James has been noticed before, especially by J. L. P. Wolmarens,[60] but Wilson elaborates upon how in contrast to the person who succumbs to this female desire, the one who withstands testing and perseveres and stands firm against desire embodies the virtues associated with ancient athletic masculinity.[61] However, just as the audience members are expected to manifest these qualities of a strong, active and heroic male self who strives for perfection, they must also remain open to receiving the "implanted word" (Jas 1:21) from a masculine father God who gave birth (Jas 1:17–18) to them. Thus the active virile self "finds completion in the realization of the passive, receptive self, the self defined vis-à-vis a masculinized God."[62] The negative characteristics associated with the feminine are now positive in that the human must passively receive God's bounteous gifts. In order to do this, however, the person is required to manifest those features typical of an ascetic male athlete. Wilson understands these human personality dynamics in James to have cosmic and social dimensions as well. The struggle in the self mirrors the community's struggle with social and economic pressures and the metaphysical conflict between good and evil. Just as the self must resist desire, the community must withstand external testings. Finally, both the self and the community must submit to the parent God who ultimately and generously offers salvation to all. Thus Wilson has provided an interesting study of how notions of gender and anthropology can shed light upon some of the theological and social dimensions of the letter.

Social and Moral Issues

Questions of how the audience is to behave dominate James, and have continued to inspire a significant amount of scholarship in the last thirty years. The following will thus focus on some of the issues that have received the most attention, but as mentioned at the beginning of this chapter, it will not be exhaustive.

Poverty and Wealth

James contains some of the strongest critique against wealth in the Christian Testament, making the letter somewhat discomfiting to some modern well-heeled readers[63] but a source of inspiration to others.[64] Through the centuries, authors have sometimes downplayed the critique of wealth in the letter or accommodated it to fit within a particular social situation. For example, the reformer John Calvin, who admired the letter, interprets James 2, in which the author criticizes those who offer the best seat in the assembly to the rich man and order the poor man to sit at their feet, not to mean that one should not respect the rich, for "it is one of the duties of courtesy, not to be neglected, to honour those who are elevated in the world."[65] Today some biblical scholars might agree with Calvin's overall view, but they are unlikely to back themselves up with the letter of James. The letter has nothing but criticism pertaining to riches, as many recent scholarly studies of the text have concluded.[66]

Pedrito Maynard-Reid's 1987 book, *Poverty and Wealth in James*,[67] was one of the first studies to focus specifically upon the letter's social milieu as it pertains to questions of poverty and wealth. His study provides detailed exegeses of three passages that deal with rich and poor: James 1:9–11; 2:1–13; and 4:13—5:6 within the social, geographic and economic contexts of the time. Maynard-Reid thinks that James reflects a direct attack upon the oppressive rich, but clearly does not advocate a violent revolution or overthrow of the wealthy.[68] Rather, God will usher in a new age in which the rich will be judged harshly for their exploitation of the poor whose cries for justice God hears and to whom God will respond. Maynard-Reid argues that James opposes the structures that allow some to become fat and live in luxury (see Jas 5:5) and states that "the principal purpose" of James's bitter denunciation of the affluent is to "give consolation and comfort to the poor and oppressed" for the poor are promised an eternal reward.[69]

James's employment of apocalyptic language in his criticism of the rich is a focus of Patrick Tiller's analysis of the text. Although Tiller thinks that eschatology functions in the letter to encourage the pious poor and threaten the rich, he is particularly interested in how apocalyptic imagery, particularly the dualism of above and below (Jas 3:15), God and the world (Jas 4:4), God and the devil (Jas 4:7; 3:15) and desire and truth (Jas 1:14–18) function with the moral teachings on poverty and wealth. Clearly James opposes the exploitation of the poor by the wealthy, but he understands this opposition within a wider framework of a dualistic cosmos in which there will be complete social reversal.[70] This reversal will include a transformation of the values of honor and shame in that the poor, who usually endured dishonor and humiliation, will be honored and inherit the kingdom (Jas 2:5). Thus James, instead of focusing upon apocalyptic revelations of the future, creates a dualistic notion of reality in which clear contrasts between two poles are created, and then locates his social critique of wealth within this reality.

Some of my work on James examines the issue of rich and poor, but with a focus upon how the letter constructs an ideology with regard to economic questions. I argue that James draws upon preexisting traditions, including LXX texts, Jewish traditions and some of the teachings of Jesus (restated in James's own words) not in order to attack a specific group of rich people, be they inside or outside of the audience, but to establish an identity among his audience of an honorable poor group that cares for the poor within it.[71] As such, James is subverting the honor ideology of the day, in which the rich are praised and lauded by some while the poor are degraded and ignored. The negative characterization of the wealthy functions as "the other" to which James's audience is contrasted, a strategy that attempts to strengthen communal solidarity. It is quite possible that external pressures to conform to some of the practices in the society in which the community exists, such as joining up with rich patrons, are threatening the cohesion and solidarity among community members. Thus in order to ward off any possible conformity at this level, James gathers various authoritative teachings and traditions in order to vilify the rich for the purpose of strengthening the identity of the audience. But James does not dwell upon the destruction of the rich precisely because his overall purpose is not to target them, but to encourage and solidify his audience as a community that honors and cares for the poor.

One of the Jewish texts with which James can be compared on the issue of rich and poor is again the *Epistle of Enoch*, which contrasts violence and falsity with justice and truth. The text includes woes against wealthy, sinful people who oppress the poor, and who will receive judgment for their actions. As in James, these people have no opportunity to repent and change their ways, but await destruction for their exploitation of the righteous. Building from Patrick Hartin's work, discussed above, John S. Kloppenborg thinks that among the writings of the early Jesus movement, James is the most similar to the *Epistle of Enoch* and that James's "catalogue of vices of the rich is remarkable for its resemblance to that of the *EpEnoch*."[72] James, like the *Epistle of Enoch*, characterizes the rich as oppressing the poor by dragging them into court and slandering their name (Jas 2:6–7; 1 Enoch 94:7), placing too much trust in their disappearing wealth (Jas 5:1–3; 1 Enoch 97:8–10) and living in luxury, exploiting workers and building wealth unjustly (Jas 4:13–17; 5:4–5; 1 Enoch 97:7–10). Unlike other texts such as Sirach or the Gospel of Luke, there is no promise that if the rich provide for the poor they will be redeemed, nor as in Kloppenborg's reading of the sayings source Q, that there can be any local cooperation between rich and poor. James, as we will discuss further below, also resists the practice of patronage (see Jas 2:1–13) whereby rich patrons will provide for clients in the community. This resistance, coupled with the repeated message that the rich will face destruction, indicates that James, like 1 Enoch, understands there to be a clear wall between the rich and poor, and does not seek any form of reconciliation or cooperation between the two.[73]

Patronage

Linked to the question of rich and poor is the topic of patronage, which many recent authors consider to be an important contextual feature relevant to understanding the letter, particularly James 2:1–13. Relationships between patrons and clients were pervasive within the Roman empire and exhibited three main features: 1) an exchange of goods and services between the two parties (often money, land or protection offered by the patron in exchange for honors, labor, etc., from the client[s]); 2) a personal liaison that could last for some time, perhaps multiple genera-tions; 3) patrons and clients of different social status.[74] The latter factor, in particular, meant that the association could easily become exploitative, with the patron asking for more and more, leaving the client very limited room to maneuver.[75]

One of the first analyses of James in the context of patronage is that of Nancy Vhymeister, who argues that the description of the rich man in James 2 conveys an image of a potential patron. For Vhymeister, the letter writer's instructions not to show favoritism to this person indicate that James is against his audi-ence attempting to gain benefits from the wealthy, even if such benefits help the community as a whole. Her study of the passage in light of patron-client relations concludes that James "is not so much condemning the rich and pronouncing himself in favor of the poor as he is advocating Christian respect for all, regardless of means or position."[76] Thus Vhymeister does not think that this passage can be employed to condemn the rich in favor of the poor, but rather, it is aimed at teaching the audience not to consider what people can do for them before deciding whether to treat them with respect.

Kloppenborg has also analyzed James 2:1–13 in the context of the patron-client model. He illustrates how the well-dressed, gold-ringed man in James 2:2 is consistent with satirical descrip-tions of rich patrons expecting bows and curtsies from clients.[77] In addition, he provides examples of nonelite ancient associations that offered honor to members who could not compete for such respect in the larger society, as well as some degree of aid and pro-tection from exploitation by the wealthy.[78] Examined in light of the latter, James's emphasis upon avoiding currying favors from affluent patrons emerges as entirely possible within the ancient world as another example of an attempt to resist the dominant models of social and economic exchange that provided many advantages to the wealthy and powerful, but were punitive to the weaker members of society.[79] In addition, Kloppenborg points to the fact that James cites Leviticus 19:18 (Jas 2:8–26) in the context of the exhortation not to show partiality. The use of Leviticus here makes the practice of favoring the wealthy just as egregious as the crimes of murder or adultery (2:8–11) thus underscoring the seriousness of the sin of partiality.[80] The audience of James is exhorted to resist the patronage of the rich and to place their trust and dependence upon their true provider, God.

Hutchinson Edgar comes to similar conclusions in his examination of James although he identifies the "poor" in the letter as itinerant social radicals of the Jesus movement who are "dishonored" by the more affluent members of the community (Jas 2:6).[81] Hutchinson Edgar takes very seriously the influence of some of Jesus' teachings on James, which we will explore in the following chapter. Based upon the role of these teachings, he also understands James within the social context of the emerging Jesus movement, and thus correlates the "poor" with the wandering radicals of that group. The chief addressees of the letter, however, are people sympathetic to the emerging Christian movement but who do not display complete dependence on God as demonstrated by their attraction to wealthy patrons and their neglect of the poor. James thus writes in order to urge them to focus their allegiance fully upon God, which will then be reflected in their day-to-day actions.

Some of the studies of patronage as a significant contextual feature of the Letter of James have argued, therefore, that the audience must resist reliance upon human patrons and trust fully in their divine patron, God. I have concurred that patronage is a key exigency of the letter, but that God is not depicted as a patron but as an ideal benefactor and friend. Prior to the late imperial period of the Roman empire, many Greeks in the eastern part of the empire had a model of benefaction, which, although it overlapped in some ways with the model of a patron, was considered to be different, at least in its ideal form. The benefactor was understood to be generous and not motivated by self-concern. The benefactor was also of assistance to others, just as friends came to each other's aid, whereas the Roman patron emerged as someone who expected honors in return for his or her services. Patrons and clients would regularly refer to one another as "friends" but in reality, they did not conform to ideal friendship at all. I have thus argued that James depicts God *in contrast to* the earthly, human patron, in order to emphasize how different God is from worldly providers, who may be called "friends," but who expect the best seats in the assembly and drag people into court (Jas 2:6). The relationship between patrons and clients, which could so easily slide into exploitation, is juxtaposed with the relationship between the faithful and God "who gives to all generously, and ungrudgingly" (Jas 1:5).[82]

Speech

This lack of a grudge should presumably also characterize the speech of the audience given the attention that James gives to talking and control of the tongue (Jas 1:19, 26–27; 3:1–12; 4:11–12). Luke Timothy Johnson has written an essay on James in light of Hellenistic discussions of brevity and found that in many ways, James is consistent with the philosophical and religious emphasis upon brevity in speech, self-control and being a good listener and a slow, careful speaker.[83] The letter differs from these comparable materials, however, insofar as the speech of humans is "qualified" by the speech of God.[84] In James speech and actions are not measured by the standards of the world but by the judgment of God and thus despite the generally pessimistic view of the tongue in the letter (see Jas 3:6–12), when James does grant positive activity to speech, he either refers to God's commands (see Jas 4:15) or exhorts activities related to speech that will strengthen the community, especially prayer (see Jas 5:13–18).[85]

William R. Baker has produced a book-length study of speech in James finding that "speech-ethics" is a major theme in the text, particularly in James 1:5–8, 19–27; 3:1–12, 18; 4:1–17; 5:9, 12–18.[86] His examination forms multiple conclusions about the nature of speech-ethics in the letter, such as the fact that control of the tongue is a spiritual concern that relates even to salvation. Speech-ethics are significant to inter-human relationships, but also to the link between humanity and God. James's emphases can be found in a variety of materials in the Mediterranean basin and in fact, Baker thinks that the "majority" of speech-ethics principles in James find parallels in background literature, although it is impossible to determine a specific influence.[87] However, James is distinctive in that he is unusually pessimistic about the tongue; he reflects upon the evil of the tongue more than other writings; he stresses the inability of people to control the tongue; and he uniquely emphasizes the human susceptibility to self-deception. Baker also joins Johnson in arguing that James is different from other ancient writings about speech in the manner in which the author so closely ties speech to "a person's spiritual and ethical development."[88] He develops these conclusions especially with regard to the human relationship with God.

Conclusion

This chapter has discussed an array of issues, theological and social, that recent scholarship has examined in the Letter of James. It is by no means a complete survey, but has attempted to cover topics that have received more attention in contemporary scholarship. As the methods of biblical scholarship develop, and as more and more people from varying contexts read and analyze James, new publications will shed fresh light on the text as they ask new questions of it.

4
JAMES AND THE SAYINGS OF JESUS

Unlike most of the texts found in the New Testament canon, James does not discuss or reflect upon the life and death of Jesus. There are only two explicit references to Jesus (Jas 1:1; 2:1) and the originality of the second one, as we have seen, has been contested by various interpreters.[1] However, it has long been noticed that James contains teachings similar to some of those attributed to Jesus, particularly those found in the Synoptic Gospels, despite the fact that there are few word-for-word parallels. James never explicitly cites Jesus or claims to be quoting from any sort of teacher, although he does quote from the Septuagint six times,[2] and gives those antecedent texts credit. Thus many questions emerge about James and the echoes of the Jesus tradition. Are there in fact parallels? If James is obtaining these teachings from another source, why does he not provide credit or cite them as authoritative, especially if the source is Jesus? Finally, if the parallels are there, how does James change them to suit the context of his letter and do the changes provide insight into the message that James is attempting to convey?

Parallels and Sources

The first question to address is what constitutes a legitimate echo or parallel with the Jesus tradition? Dean B. Deppe's 1989 dissertation has addressed this issue and provides a very helpful history of scholarship on the relationship between James and the sayings of Jesus.[3] Deppe includes an appendix that lists the number of correlations between James and the Synoptic Gospels for which scholars have made a case since the year 1833. Some authors have argued for as many as 65 while others limit it to 4 or 5![4] This means that on average authors have argued for 18 parallels, a striking number when one compares the single, short Letter of James to the collection of undisputed Pauline letters, in which there are perhaps 24 correlations.[5] Moreover, almost every verse in James has been addressed as having a possible association with traditions connected to Jesus.

Deppe thinks that there are 8 "conscious allusions" to the Synoptic Gospels in James, which he lists as: James 1:5 = Matthew 7:7 and Luke 11:9 (ask and you will receive); James 4:2c–3 = Matthew 7:7 and Luke 11:9 (ask and you will receive); James 2:5 = Luke 6:20b and Matthew 5:3 (the kingdom belongs to the poor); James 5:2–3a = Matthew 6:19–20 and Luke 12:33b (do not store up wealth); James 4:9 = Luke 6:21, 25b (those who laugh will mourn); James 5:1 = Luke 6:24 (woe to the rich); James 5:12 = Matthew 5:33–37 (on oaths and truth-telling); James 4:10 = Matthew 23:12 and Luke 14:11 and Luke 18:14b (the humble are exalted).[6] In addition to these allusions to specific sayings of Jesus, Deppe finds ethical themes from Jesus' preaching that James uses as "raw material for the church's ethical paraenesis."[7] These include joy in tribulation (Jas 1:2; 5:10–11a); faith and doubting (Jas 1:6); teachings against anger (Jas 1:19–20); hearing and doing and faith and action (Jas 1:22–25; Jas 2:14); the commandment to love (Jas 2:8); an emphasis upon mercy (Jas 2:13); serving God versus loving the world (Jas 4:4); refraining from judging (Jas 4:11–12; 5:9); and the notion that those who persevere in trials will receive blessings (Jas 1:12; 5:10–11a).[8] According to Deppe, this number of allusions to the teachings and ideas of Jesus from the Synoptic tradition is not insignificant in the short Letter of James, but he also remarks that James does not contain the most allusions to the sayings of Jesus among ancient Christian documents. The Book of Revelation, in his view, contains about 25 allusions, Paul's letters contain between 8 and 24 Jesus sayings, while 12 traditions associated with the teaching of Jesus reverberate throughout 1 Peter.[9]

If we posit that James is referring to a body of Jesus tradition, what was his source for such material? Obviously questions of the date of the letter factor in here, for if it is an early text, that is, pre-60 CE, it would not have known the Synoptic Gospels which are usually dated from the 60s to the 80s. Indeed, I am not aware of any scholars in the past thirty years who argue that James is directly dependent upon the gospels. For Deppe, James is a witness to the sayings of Jesus that are "in the air."[10] There is no clear indication that James knew the Synoptics, nor that he knew of the pre-synoptic Q sayings source. Deppe also thinks that the best explanation of the authorship of James is that it emerged from James of Jerusalem, although Deppe does not argue stridently for this but states that authentic authorship is "probably a preferable solution" since it has survived as an explanation for some time.[11] Thus the Letter of James independently adapts the teachings of Jesus to new situations. Jesus' wisdom serves as a type of "thematic raw material for the church's ethical paraenesis."[12]

A recent joint piece by Luke Timothy Johnson and Wesley H. Wachob examines the Letter of James and the sayings of Jesus, but it limits its analysis to 4 of Deppe's conscious allusions, namely James 1:5; 2:5; 4:2c–3; 5:12, and two others: James 2:8 and 2:13. Johnson and Wachob think that the latter two examples do not sufficiently demonstrate a direct knowledge of the Jesus tradition although the teachings might have emerged as a result of an awareness of Jesus' teachings. The prior four, however, indicate "not simply an echo of Jesus' teaching but a specific use of his words...."[13] Thus there is a clear link to Jesus' teachings. Johnson, as we saw in an earlier chapter, believes that the letter was written by James, the brother of Jesus, while Wachob thinks that an anonymous author wrote in the name of James. Both, however, conclude that the text draws upon a pre-synoptic version of Jesus' teachings, which supports, in their view, a relatively early dating of the letter.[14]

Patrick Hartin devoted a doctoral dissertation and subsequent monograph to examining the relationship between James and the Q sayings of Jesus. He lists 26 possible links between James and the Synoptic Gospels, the vast majority coming from the Sermon on the Mount.[15] All of the links between James and the Synoptic traditions that Hartin examines will not be elaborated here, nor have scholars unanimously found all of Hartin's arguments for parallels convincing, but his exploration of a possible relationship between James and a form of Q has considerably advanced the discussion of the relationship between James and the sayings of Jesus. In particular, Hartin notices how James seems to know the form of a Q tradition that was developing within the Matthean community. More specifically, he sees parallels such as James 2:13 and Matthew 5:7 (Q 6:36), but he does not see any evidence that James was familiar with the actual gospel writer's redaction of these sayings, but rather pre-gospel manifestations of them as they were evolving in the Matthean context.[16] For Hartin, this all means that James is somewhere between Q and Matthew. As he writes: "The knowledge that James has of the traditions and sources that go into the Gospel of Matthew is such that the epistle situates itself before the codification of these sources took place within the Gospel of Matthew."[17] James freely adapts this Q tradition to his own situation and as Hartin points out, makes no distinction between the teachings of Jesus and the teachings of James. Finally, for Hartin, the fact that James betrays an awareness of this pre-synoptic layer of Jesus' teachings supports the notion that James must be a very early text, indeed one of the earliest texts in the New Testament.

James's Adaptation of Jesus Traditions

We have only surveyed a few authors above, but it is reasonable to say that in general, scholars agree that there is a relationship between James and the teaching traditions associated with Jesus. The number of links between Jesus' sayings and the Letter of James is still debated, but the discussion of the issue tends to focus more on the nature of the parallels between the two. There still may be no consensus on the date or authorship of James, as we saw in an earlier chapter, but even most of those scholars who push for a late date of composition do not argue for Jacobean dependence upon the Synoptic Gospels. But if James knew of some traditions of Jesus in some form, either oral or written, what did he do to them as he incorporated them into his letter? How did James alter the sayings of Jesus to fit the context of his particular letter? Recent scholarship has examined this issue.

Richard Bauckham, who as we have already seen thinks that James was written by James of Jerusalem, has found parallels between James's practice of "creative re-expression"[18] of Jesus' teachings and the deuterocanonical Book of Sirach, written by Ben Sira. Ben Sira does to Proverbs, a source from which he drew insights and wisdom, what James does to some of the teachings of Jesus. Ben Sira never quotes Proverbs, and as Bauckham points out, only three times does he reproduce it word-for-word, and even there, it is not even half a verse.[19] As Ben Sira understood himself to have inherited the accumulated wisdom from a long line of wise teachers, he creatively adapts this prior wisdom to suit his own context. Thus one can compare Proverbs 22:8: "Whoever sows injustice will reap calamity, and the rod of his anger will fail," to Sirach 7:3: "Do not sow in the furrows of injustice, and you will not reap a sevenfold crop" and notice the parallel ideas and vocabulary, but observe how Ben Sira has become a "*creative* exponent of the tradition, interpreting it in fresh formulations of his own."[20] In addition, Ben Sira draws upon other literary traditions, both biblical and nonbiblical, but he does not quote them exactly, nor attribute his wisdom to these prior texts. Rather, in the tradition of the sages, he modifies and reformulates this *old* wisdom to fit his context. Indeed according to Bauckham this is the role of the sage: "to make the old wisdom his own and to express it as his own wisdom."[21]

James, like Ben Sira, draws from traditional Jewish wisdom sources without citing them and makes them his own. Bauckham provides several examples of wisdom teachings on anger (Sir 5:11; Prov 29:20; Prov 18:13; Sir 20:7a; Eccles 7:9a; Prov 16:32a) that James then creatively adapts such that he is not only continuing on the tradition but making a contribution to it as well, with his teachings on being quick to hear, slow to speak and slow to anger (Jas 1:19). James has not simply copied these prior teachings about anger, but mined them as sources of inspiration so that he can then create his own wise proverb on the topic.[22]

This practice continues with some of the teachings of Jesus such as James 2:5b, which in Bauckham's view has re-expressed Jesus' blessing of the poor with its stress on how God has chosen the poor in the world to be rich in faith and heirs of the kingdom that God has promised to those who love God (Matt 5:3; Luke 6:20). James has not *alluded* to Jesus' teaching here; he has been inspired by it to create his own wisdom. In doing so, he has artfully conveyed the Jewish tradition that the pious poor are models of faith because in their lack of material resources, they demonstrate "utter dependence upon God which is what true faith is."[23] Likewise in 2:13, James crafts wise aphorisms about how judgment will be without mercy to the one who has not shown mercy, and how mercy triumphs over judgment. These teachings do not allude to teachings of Jesus, but in Bauckham's view, reveal an awareness of how Jesus had made traditional Jewish wisdom his own (see Matt 7:1–2; Matt 5:7; Luke 6:37a, 38b) as similar sorts of declarations about mercy and judgment appear in earlier literature such as Sirach 28:1–4 and Proverbs 17:5. Thus James, aware of these earlier Jewish traditions and of how Jesus had adapted them for his specific purposes, drew from both the wisdom of the Jewish tradition and Jesus' exemplary practice of re-expressing it, and created his own version of the teaching appropriate to his own historical and literary context.[24]

For Bauckham, it is not necessary that James's audience recognize the teachings of Jesus in James' wisdom. James does not quote or allude to the sayings of Jesus, but finds inspiration in Jesus' teaching that prompts him to create his own proverbs and aphorisms that both reflect the Jewish wisdom tradition as well as Jesus' insights. Bauckham understands both the wisdom of Jesus and that of James to be thoroughly Jewish, but also somewhat novel in both teachers' emphasis upon solidarity with the poor and the reversal of status hierarchies. James does not allude to Jesus' teachings, as stated earlier, but he does find in Jesus' specific appropriation of Jewish wisdom an inspiration and principal guide for his own appropriation of these traditions.[25] However, the wisdom of James is clearly that: the wisdom of James. Although various influences have played central roles in motivating James to create his wisdom teachings in the manner that he has, it is not necessary for the audience to notice that such wisdom contains specific references to the teachings of Jesus in order for them to appreciate James's particular and wise voice.

Bauckham's approach to James and the teachings of Jesus differs from that of Wesley Hiram Wachob, whose work we have encountered already in the previous chapter on structure and rhetoric. Wachob focuses specifically upon James 2:5 as a Jacobean performance of a saying of Jesus. For Wachob, the saying best reflects a Jesus tradition from a form of Q that was developing within the Matthean milieu, but which predates Matthew's gospel. Wachob agrees with Hans Dieter Betz's argument that there was a very early pre-Matthean form of the Sermon on the Mount, and that there is some sort of textual connection between this sermon and James.[26] James consciously uses Jesus' beatitude regarding the blessing of the poor according to the practice of "progymnastic recitation" a Greek rhetorical practice of elaborating on particular themes by activating, in part, previous texts.[27] It is important to Wachob, unlike Bauckham, that James 2:5 is a clear allusion to a teaching of Jesus and he thinks that this is the case because in James 2:5, like the other texts that contain this teaching (Matt 5:3; Luke 6:20b; *Gos. Thom* 54; Pol. *Phil* 2:3) the common denominators of "the kingdom" being promised to "the poor" appear. Moreover, in Wachob's view, the reference to Jesus Christ in James 2:1, which he deems authentic to the letter, is an additional signal that Jesus' teaching is in view.[28]

Thus unlike Bauckham who argues that James has been inspired by Jesus' overall appropriation and re-expression of Jewish wisdom, but who thinks that James has created his own collection of wise teachings that do not require a recognition of Jesus' teachings therein, Wachob believes it important that the audience notice that James has alluded to Jesus' teaching about the kingdom belonging to the poor and that this allusion constitutes part of the rhetorical power of James's teaching here. Moreover, as the letter introduces its speaker as a spokesperson for God and the Lord Jesus Christ, it indicates that there is a like-minded purpose between God and Jesus. James 2:5 then uses a well-known saying of Jesus as an example that reveals God's concern and care for the poor; an example that offers a reminder to James's listeners that God's will and Jesus' will are one. Moreover, because in Wachob's view the audience would have recognized James 2:5 as a teaching of Jesus, the use of it here enhances the authority of the speaker, who presents himself as James the Lord's brother (although Wachob thinks the letter is pseudonymous) for it indicates that the wisdom of Jesus and the wisdom of James are one and the same and are consistent with the wisdom of God.[29]

John S. Kloppenborg concurs with Wachob that the recognition of Jesus' voice within the letter of James is important for the rhetorical power of the document. Kloppenborg builds from the studies of Deppe, Hartin, Bauckham, Wachob and others but he goes further in examining how and why James is employing such teachings. We engaged with Kloppenborg's work on this topic briefly in the earlier chapter on structure and rhetoric, but here we can a little more fully describe his analysis.

In agreement with Hartin and Wachob, Kloppenborg thinks that James had some Jesus traditions available to him in a pre-Matthean Q form, but Kloppenborg puzzles over why there is little verbal agreement and why James fails to acknowledge Jesus as the original source of such teachings. He thus turns to Greek writers, in particular those who practiced the art of paraphrasing an earlier teacher's wisdom. It was reasonably common for Greek authors to paraphrase a preexisting text, thus accounting for a lack of word-for-word agreement, and not to attribute the previous teaching to an author, but to represent it as the work of the "paraphrast." This process of putting another person's ideas into one's own version is what the rhetorical experts called *aemulatio* and generally it was assumed that the audience who heard or read such paraphrases recognized the source for them.[30] The differences between the primary source and the paraphrase are not due to the creativity that inevitably occurs during oral transmission, but are consciously crafted by the paraphrast. Thus Kloppenborg explores how some of the passages in James, which many think find their origins in the teachings of Jesus, have been altered and shaped to suit James's overall aims according to some of the procedures developed by those who practiced *aemulatio*.

Like Wachob, Kloppenborg explores James 2:5 as a "recitation" of a Jesus saying from a stage of the Q tradition. However, he goes further than Wachob, who focuses primarily upon how the saying functions within James 2:1–13, which Wachob has argued conforms to an elaboration of a theme exercise found among ancient rhetoricians. Kloppenborg examines the details of how James paraphrases the tradition from Q 6:20b ("blessed are the poor, for yours is the kingdom of God") to suit the elaboration of a theme in James 2:1–13. He argues that the overall aim of James in this segment is to demonstrate that acts of partiality "are against self-interest (vv. 5–7) and amount to a violation of the Torah (vv. 8–11)."[31] As we observed in chapter 2, Kloppenborg claims that the aim of the verses is to show that the values that the audience claims to hold are not supported by the ways in which they behave. James thus elaborates Q's "the poor" to the "poor in the world" in order to ally the poor with one of the "main binary oppositions of the letter, between the (actual) rich and (actual) poor."[32] According to Kloppenborg, James wants his addressees to be sympathetic towards these poor and against the rich. Therefore, James further elaborates Q 6:20b to say that the poor are rich in faith, that they will inherit the kingdom and that the kingdom is for those who love God. These elaborations are intended to appeal to what the addressees believe about themselves and thus the additions would serve to identify them with the poor. James does not stop but continues on in James 2:6 to say "but you have dishonored the poor man," which effectively demonstrates to the audience that when it shows partiality to the wealthy it not only dishonors the poor man, but goes against the audience's own self-interest insofar as the audience identifies with the poor.[33] Thus Kloppenborg accounts for the specific changes to the original saying of Jesus by showing how these changes support James in his argument against partiality for the rich. Unlike Bauckham, but consistent with Wachob, Kloppenborg points out that this practice of *aemulatio* presumes that the audience will recognize the source of the paraphrase. Therefore James, in using Jesus' teaching as a source, effectively aligns himself with the "*ethos* of the original speaker" while simultaneously allowing the addressees to "appreciate the artistry of paraphrase and application of the old maxim to a new rhetorical situation."[34]

In a more recent essay, Kloppenborg continues his examination of *aemulatio* in James through analyses of other texts that many think find their source in the teachings of Jesus, such as James 4:3–4 (Q 16:13) and James 5:1, 2‑3 (Q 6:24; 12:33–34).[35] In each he shows how James's specific changes to the source text can be accounted for, given the social and rhetorical aims of the segment of the letter and according to ancient practices of paraphrase. Thus James 5:1, 2–3, which Kloppenborg concurs with Johnson is part of the larger segment of James 4:13—5:6 that focuses upon arrogance introduced by 4:11–12, addresses the "brothers" (Jas 4:11) who are in the community. This accounts for why the "woe" of Q 6:24 is changed to "come now" in James 4:13. Unlike many commentators who argue that James 4:11—5:6 attacks those who are external to the audience, Kloppenborg thinks that this unit does not place the rich on the outside unlike

James 1:10, which does. However, the focus of the attack is not so much on the rich themselves, but on their wealth, their material goods.[36] Q 12:33–34 becomes the rationale for the catastrophe that befalls those who store up treasures for themselves in James 5:1–2. As Kloppenborg observes, some of the key "lexemes" in Q, such as "treasure" and "moths," are preserved in James.[37] However, James elaborates Q's "treasures" to include wealth, likely in the form of agricultural foodstuffs because they can rot, clothing and precious metals such as gold and silver, which probably refer to ornaments and jewelry. For Kloppenborg, James has shifted the "social register" of wealth from the country to the city, where clothing and outward ornamentation are the most significant symbols of wealth. The argument, overall, is about the "intrinsically corrupting nature of wealth" and although James 5:5 refers to the coming eschatological judgment, James 5:1–3, like Q 12:16–20, expresses the opposition between the priorities of the wealthy, who store up treasures for themselves, and God's perspective of wealth, which is that it is transitory and of no worth.[38]

Kloppenborg's work here constitutes a significant contribution to the study of James on this issue for it not only cements the notion that James was rhetorically sophisticated and provides further evidence that James did indeed draw from the Jesus tradition, but in its introduction of the notion of *aemulatio* it provides a concrete historical model that one can apply to James in order to illuminate how the letter is transforming antecedent texts. Thus scholars can now systematically test other parallels between James and the sayings of Jesus using *aemulatio* as a controlled guide for determining more precisely how James is transforming earlier traditions to suit his own purposes.

Conclusion

Although the connections between the teachings of Jesus and those of James have been recognized for some time, significant progress has been made not only regarding what form of Jesus' teachings James may have been aware of, namely some iteration of Q, but also the manner in which James adapts Jesus' teachings to suit the context of his letter. Significant disagreements persist, such as whether or not it matters if James wants his audience to know that he is alluding to a teaching of Jesus, but more attention to rhetoric and particularly, the art of *aemulatio* may aid in clarifying the importance of recognizing the teachings of Jesus embedded within the Letter of James.

It is appropriate to end this book with this particular chapter for the topic of James and the sayings of Jesus constitutes, in my view, one of the most intriguing aspects of this short letter. Not only does work in this area aid in understanding the themes and purpose of the letter itself, it has significant historical implications. For example, more and more scholars are concurring that James knew some form of Q, which indicates that studying James may be useful for other topics, such as Q studies and the analysis of the literary relationship between Matthew, Mark and Luke, commonly referred to as the Synoptic Problem. Examination of the sayings of Jesus in James is a factor in the consideration of the tricky issue of the date of the letter and it should be obvious that it contributes to further appreciation of James as a rhetorically sophisticated document. Moreover, much of the work in this area is very recent, and thus we will likely witness some exciting further developments in the next ten to twenty years. As this brief survey of issues has attempted to demonstrate, research upon the Letter of James has experienced resurgence in the past three decades. James scholarship now has a very firm foothold, and I anticipate that it will continue to make significant steps forward in the years to come.

NOTES

Introduction

1. For an introduction to recent scholarship on these letters, which include James, 1 and 2 Peter, Jude, 1, 2 and 3 John, see Philip B. Harner, *What Are They Saying About the Catholic Epistles?* (New York/Mahwah, NJ: Paulist, 2004).

2. For a recent study of scholarship on the figure of James, see Matti Myllykoski, "James the Just in History and Tradition: Perspectives of Past and Present Scholarship (Part I)," *CBR* 5.1 (2006) 73–122.

Chapter One: Genre, Structure and Rhetoric of James

1. Martin Dibelius, *James. A Commentary on the Epistle of James*, rev. Heinrich Greeven; trans. Michael A. Williams (Philadelphia: Fortress, 1976) 2–3.

2. See Leo G. Perdue, "Paraenesis and the Epistle of James," *ZNW* 72 (1981) 241–56; "The Death of the Sage and Moral Exhortation: From Ancient Near Eastern Instructions to Graeco-Roman Paraenesis," *Semeia* 50 (1990) 81–109.

3. Peter H. Davids, *The Epistle of James: A Commentary on the Greek Text* (Grand Rapids: Eerdmans, 1982). See also, Todd C.

Penner, "The Epistle of James in Current Research," *Currents in Research: Biblical Studies* 7 (1999) 257–308.

4. Davids, *Epistle of James*, 25.

5. Ernst Baasland, "Literarische Form, Thematik und geschichtliche Einordung des Jakobusbriefes,"*ANRW* 2.25.5 (1988) 3655.

6. Patrick J. Hartin, *James* (Collegeville, MN: Liturgical Press, 2003) 15.

7. John G. Gammie, "Paraenetic Literature: Toward the Morphology of a Secondary Genre," *Semeia* 50 (1990) 41–77.

8. David Hutchinson Edgar, *Has God Not Chosen the Poor? The Social Setting of the Epistle of James* (Sheffield: Sheffield Academic Press, 2001) 17.

9. Wesley Hiram Wachob, *The Voice of Jesus in the Social Rhetoric of James* (Cambridge: Cambridge University Press, 2000) 52. Wachob builds off of the work of Klaus Berger, *Formgeschichte des Neuen Testament* (Heidelberg: Quelle & Meyer, 1984) 147.

10. Wiard Popkes, "James and Paraenesis," in *Texts and Contexts. Biblical Texts in Their Textual and Situational Contexts*, Tord Fornberg and David Hellholm, eds. (Oslo: Scandinavian University Press, 1995) 548–49.

11. David E. Aune, *The New Testament in Its Literary Environment* (Philadelphia: Westminster, 1987) 170.

12. Fred O. Francis, "The Form and Function of the Opening and Closing Paragraphs of James and 1 John," *ZNW* 61 (1970) 110–26.

13. For example, Philemon 4–7 contains a double opening statement and 1 John ends very abruptly.

14. See Aune, *The New Testament,* 171, reference to the letters of Apollonius, a second-century CE grammarian.

15. Francis, "Form and Function," 126.

16. Manabu Tsuji, *Glaube zwischen Vollkommenheit und Verweltlichung: Eine Untersuchung zur literarischen Gestalt und zur inhaltlichen Kohärenz des Jakobusbriefes* (Tübingen: J. C. B. Mohr [Siebeck] 1997).

17. Karl-Wilhelm Niebuhr, "Der Jakobusbrief im Licht frühjüdischer Diasporabriefe," *NTS* 44 (1998) 420–43. For some

of these texts, see Dennis Pardee, *Handbook of Ancient Hebrew Letters* (Chico, CA: Scholars, 1982) 186–89.

18. Davids, "Palestinian Traditions in the Epistle of James," in *James the Just and Christian Origins*, Bruce Chilton and Craig A. Evans, eds. (Leiden: Brill, 1999) 41.

19. S. R. Llewellyn, "The Prescript of James," *NovT* 39 (1997) 385–93.

20. Of note here is the observation that Sophie Laws's commentary on James (*The Epistle of James* [London: Adam and Charles Black, 1980] 6) grants that James is a literary letter, but "the structure of the writing is loose."

21. See Mark E. Taylor, "Recent Scholarship on the Structure of James," *Currents in Biblical Research* 3.1 (2004) 91–92, who outlines the studies of E. Pfeiffer ("Der Zusammendhang des Jakobusbriefes," *TSK* 1 [1850] 163–80) and H. J. Cladder ("Die Anfang des Jakobusbriefes," *ZKT* 28 [1904] 37–57).

22. Francis, "Form and Function," 118. Francis provides a thorough discussion of various comparable documents from antiquity that use this twofold structure in their opening sections.

23. Ibid., 118.

24. Ibid., 125.

25. Ibid., 126.

26. Ibid., 125.

27. Peter H. Davids, "The Epistle of James in Modern Discussion," *ANRW* 2.25.5 (1988) 3629, n. 28.

28. Ibid., 27–28.

29. Ibid., 26.

30. James M. Reese, "The Exegete as Sage: Hearing the Message of James," *BTB* 12 (1982) 83.

31. Robert B. Crotty, "The Literary Structure of James," *ABR* 40 (1992) 55.

32. Patrick J. Hartin, *James and the Q Sayings of Jesus* (Sheffield: JSOT Press, 1991) 30–31.

33. Patrick J. Hartin, *James* (Collegeville, MN: Liturgical Press, 2003) 28.

34. Ibid.

35. Ibid., 29.

36. Taylor, "Recent Scholarship," 95.

37. Luke Timothy Johnson, *The Letter of James* (New York: Doubleday, 1995) 14.

38. Ibid.

39. Timothy Cargal, *Restoring the Diaspora: Discursive Structure and Purpose in the Epistle of James* (Atlanta: Scholars, 1993) 45.

40. Robert W. Wall, *Community of the Wise. The Letter of James* (Valley Forge, PA: Trinity, 1997) 43.

41. Ibid., 73.

42. Ibid., 74.

43. Ibid., 273.

44. Todd C. Penner, *The Epistle of James and Eschatology. Re-reading an Ancient Christian Letter* (Sheffield: Sheffield Academic Press, 1996) 143.

45. Ibid., 144–45.

46. Ibid., 157.

47. Ibid., 158–59.

48. François Vouga, *L'Épître de Saint Jacques* (Geneva: Labor et Fides, 1984) 19–20.

49. Ralph P. Martin, *James* (Waco, TX: Word Books, 1988) cii.

50. James B. Adamson, *James. The Man and His Message* (Grand Rapids: Eerdmans, 1989) 92. As Adamson puts it: "In our view, every principle and theme in the rest of the Epistle of James is repeated, expanded, or derived from 1:2–18, on the Christian mind (what are we to believe and feel?), and from 1:19–27, on Christian conduct (what are we to do?). There is more unity of thought in James than we sometimes suppose."

51. Martin Klein, *"Ein vollkommenes Werk": Vollkommenheit, Gesetz und Gericht als theologische Themen des Jakobusbriefes* (Stuttgart: Kohlhammer, 1995) 33–41. Douglas Moo (*The Letter of James* [Leicester: Apollos / Grand Rapids: Eerdmans, 2000] 46) thinks that "spiritual wholeness" or "perfection" is a "central concern" of James but he does not emphasize the role of Jas 1 in developing this concern; rather Jas 4:4–10.

52. Richard Bauckham, *James. Wisdom of James, Disciple of Jesus the Sage* (London: Routledge, 1999) 73.

53. Kenneth D. Tollefson, "The Epistle of James as Dialectical Discourse," *BTB* 21 (1997) 69.

54. Mark E. Taylor, "Recent Scholarship," 11. See also, Mark E. Taylor, *A Text-Linguistic Investigation into the Discourse Structure of James* (London: T & T Clark, 2006).

55. Wiard Popkes (*Der Brief des Jakobus* [Leipzig: Evangelische Verlagsanstalt, 2001] 54–57), for example, thinks that James is shaped more by the traditions that it incorporates into itself, and not a literary structure.

56. Burton L. Mack, *Rhetoric and the New Testament* (Minneapolis: Fortress, 1990) 31.

57. For discussion of this issue, see Duane F. Watson and Alan J. Hauser, *Rhetorical Criticism of the Bible. A Comprehensive Bibliography with Notes on History and Method* (Leiden: Brill, 1994) 121.

58. Aune, *The New Testament*, 160. For more discussion of the influence of rhetorical theory on letter writing, see F. W. Hughes, *Early Christian Rhetoric and 2 Thessalonians* (Sheffield: Sheffield Academic Press, 1989). Hughes discusses how the letters of Demosthenes were written according to ancient rhetorical rules.

59. Lloyd Bitzer, "The Rhetorical Situation," *Philosophy and Rhetoric* 1 (1968) 1–14.

60. Ibid., 8.

61. Baasland ("Literarische Form," 3648) points out that early twentieth-century scholars J. D. Schulze, C. G. Küchler, C. G. Wilke and J. A. Bengel all used rhetoric, albeit somewhat unsystematically, in their studies of James.

62. Lauri Thurén, "Risky Rhetoric in James?" *NovT* 37 (1995) 264.

63. For a discussion of these types of rhetoric, see George A. Kennedy, *A New History of Classical Rhetoric* (Princeton: Princeton University Press, 1994) 58–59.

64. Thurén, "Risky Rhetoric," 176–77. Thurén points out that it is difficult to determine the species of James.

65. Wilhelm Wuellner, "Der Jakobusbrief im Licht der Rhetorik und Textpragmatik," *LB* 43 (1978) 5–66.

66. Ibid., 12–13.

67. Cicero (*De Inventione* 1.25 [trans H. M. Hubbell; Cambridge, MA: Harvard / London: Heinemann, 1949]) says that the *exordium* must "contain everything which contributes to dignity,

because the best thing to do is that which especially commends the speaker to his audience. It should contain very little brilliance, vivacity, or finish of style, because these give rise to a suspicion of preparation and excessive ingenuity."

68. Wuellner, "Der Jakobusbrief," 41.

69. A *narratio* is not required in deliberative rhetoric, but can appear, but it is very important in legal or judicial rhetoric, in which a judgment must be made about an event or person in the past.

70. Wuellner, "Der Jakobusbrief," 37.

71. Ibid., 36.

72. John H. Elliott, "The Epistle of James in Rhetorical and Social Scientific Perspective. Holiness-Wholeness and Patterns of Replication," *BTB* 23 (1993) 79.

73. Ernst Baasland, *Jakobsbrevet* (Uppsala: EFS, 1992) 178. Baasland's treatment of the rhetorical structure of James in this commentary differs somewhat from his earlier work (see Baasland, "Literarische Form," 3655–56) in which he presents only one *propositio* in Jas 1:19–27.

74. Baasland, *Jakobusbrevet*, 177.

75. Hubert Frankenmölle, "Das semantische Netz des Jakobusbriefes. Zur Einheit eines umstritten Briefes," *BZ* 34 (1990) 175. Also see his more recent commentary, *Der Brief des Jakobus* (Gütersloh: Gütersloher Verlaghaus, 1994).

76. This structure is clearly illustrated in Frankenmölle, "Das semantische," 193.

77. Thurén, "Risky Rhetoric," 282.

78. Ibid., 278.

79. Hartin argues for such a pattern in a number of sections of James, including 3:13—4:10 (*James*, 203–16). I also independently argued for this rhetorical structure in this section of the letter (see Alicia Batten, *Unworldly Friendship: "The Epistle of Straw" Reconsidered* [doctoral dissertation; University of St. Michael's College, 2000] 167–201).

80. J. D. N. van der Westhuizen, "Stylistic Techniques and their Functions in James 2:14–26," *Neot* 25 (1991) 105–6.

81. Baasland ("Literarische Form," 3649–54) and others have also noticed the use of diatribe in James.

82. Stanley Stowers, "The Diatribe," in *Greco-Roman Literature and the New Testament*, David E. Aune, ed. (Atlanta: Scholars, 1988) 75.

83. Duane F. Watson, "James 2 in Light of Greco-Roman Schemes of Argumentation," *NTS* 39 (1993) 121.

84. Duane F. Watson, "The Rhetoric of James 3:1–12 and a Classical Pattern of Argumentation," *NovT* 35 (1993) 48.

85. Dibelius, *James*, 182.

86. See Duane F. Watson, "A Reassessment of the Rhetoric of the Epistle of James and Its Implications for Christian Origins," in *Reading James with New Eyes. Methodological Reassessments of the Letter of James*, Robert L. Webb and John S. Kloppenborg, eds. (London: T & T Clark, 2007) 99–120.

87. Bauckham, *James*, 62.

88. Ibid., 30.

89. Wachob, *Voice of Jesus*, 70.

90. Ibid., 76.

91. Ibid., 85.

92. Wachob (ibid., 120–21) builds off the work of Vernon K. Robbins ("Writing as a Rhetorical Act in Plutarch and the Gospels," in *Persuasive Artistry: Studies in New Testament Rhetoric in Honor of George A. Kennedy*, Duane F. Watson, ed., [Sheffield: JSOT Press, 1991] 157–86), who examines the textbooks of the first-century Greek author, Theon.

93. See, for example, John Painter, "The Power of Words: Rhetoric in James and Paul," in *The Missions of James, Peter and Paul. Tensions in Early Christianity*, Bruce Chilton and Craig Evans, eds., NovTSupp 115 (2005) 253–73. See also, Wesley H. Wachob, "The Languages of 'Household' and 'Kingdom' in the Letter of James: A Socio-Rhetorical Study," in *Reading James with New Eyes. Methodological Reassessments of the Letter of James*, Robert L. Webb and Johns S. Kloppenborg, eds. (London: T & T Clark, 2007) 151–68.

94. John S. Kloppenborg, "The Reception of Jesus Traditions in James," in *The Catholic Epistles and the Tradition*, J. Schlosser, ed. (Leuven: Peeters, 2004) 139.

95. Ibid., 141.

96. See also, John S. Kloppenborg Verbin, "Patronage Avoidance in James," *HTS* 55 (1999) 755–94.

97. See Hartin, *James*, 181–90.

Chapter Two: Authorship and Audience of James

1. See Ralph P. Martin, *James* (Waco, TX: Word Books, 1988) xxxiii–xxxiv.

2. Patrick J. Hartin, *James of Jerusalem. Heir to Jesus of Nazareth* (Collegeville, MN: Michael Glazier Books, 2004) 1–43. There have been three main ways of understanding references to Jesus' siblings in the gospels, namely the Epiphanian view wherein the brothers and sisters of Jesus are products of a previous marriage of Joseph; the Helvidian theory whereby the siblings are Jesus' actual blood brothers and sisters; and the Hieronymian theory that understands them to be cousins of Jesus. Obviously the Helvidian theory does not cohere with official Roman Catholic teaching although it is the view held by most Protestants and some Roman Catholic scholars.

3. Josephus, *Ant.* 20. 200.

4. Eusebius, *Hist. eccl.* 2.23.20.

5. Ibid., 2.23.4–18.

6. Ibid., 2.1.3–5.

7. Parts of this gospel are preserved in Jerome, *Vir. ill.* 2.

8. *Ps.-Clem* 1.1.

9. *Gos. Thom.* 12.

10. *Prot. Jas.* 9.2.

11. *Prot. Jas.* 25.1.

12. Today the text is not thought to be by James because it is not understood to have been written until at least the middle of the second century CE. The fact that the text claims to be by James, however, indicates that the name held authority within the early church.

13. See the collection of essays edited by Matt Jackson-McCabe, *Jewish Christianity Reconsidered. Rethinking Ancient Groups and Texts* (Minneapolis: Fortress, 2007).

14. John Painter, *Just James: The Brother of Jesus in History and Tradition* (Columbia: University of South Carolina Press, 1997); Pierre Antoine Bernheim, *James, Brother of Jesus*, trans. John Bowden (London: SCM Press, 1997); Bruce B. Chilton and Craig A. Evans, eds., *James the Just and Christian Origins* (Leiden: E. J. Brill, 1999); Bruce B. Chilton and Jacob Neusner, eds., *The Brother of Jesus. James the Just and His Mission* (Louisville: Westminster/John Knox Press, 2001).

15. Matti Myllykoski, "James the Just in History and Tradition: Perspectives of Past and Present Scholarship (Part I)," *Currents in Biblical Research* 5.1 (2006) 112.

16. Origen, *Comm. Rom.* IV, 8.

17. It is worth noting that Origen refers to James as "scripture" in *Comm. Matt.* XIX, 61, but that his reference to something as "scripture" does not necessarily mean that it is canonical. This point is made by Robert W. Wall, "A Unifying Theology of the Catholic Epistles. A Canonical Approach," in *The Catholic Epistles and the Tradition*, J. Schlosser, ed., (Leuven: Peeters, 2004) 52, n. 24.

18. Eusebius, *Hist. eccl.* 3.25.3.

19. Eusebius, *Hist. eccl.* 2.23.25. Here Eusebius says that James is disputed because few of the ancients quote it, as is the case with Jude. However, he says that these letters are used publicly in most churches.

20. Hilary of Poitiers, *De Trin.* IV, 8.26.

21. Laws, *The Epistle of James*, 22–26.

22. Luke Timothy Johnson, *Brother of Jesus, Friend of God* (Grand Rapids: Eerdmans, 2004) 91–96.

23. Ibid., 84–100.

24. Jonathan P. Yates, "The Reception of the Epistle of James in the Latin West: Did Athanasius Play a Role?" in *The Catholic Epistles and the Tradition*, 273–88.

25. For a discussion of Luther's view, see James Hardy Ropes, *A Critical and Exegetical Commentary on the Epistle of St. James* (Edinburgh: T & T Clark, 1916) 104–9.

26. Laws (*James*, 40) points to Acts 15:13–21, which depicts James presiding over a council dealing with what ritual practices Gentile converts should follow.

27. Dibelius, *James*, 18; Laws, *James*, 37, 41.

28. Sophie Laws, "James, Epistle of," *AB* 3 (1992) 624.

29. Ibid., 622.

30. Popkes, *Der Brief*, 69.

31. Ibid., 43.

32. Wachob, *The Voice of Jesus*, 132.

33. See chapter five of this book for Wachob's discussion of James and Q.

34. Wachob, *The Voice of Jesus*, 201.

35. Ibid.

36. Penner, *The Epistle of James and Eschatology*, 73.

37. Ibid., 281.

38. Wall, "A Unifying Theology," 54.

39. See ibid., 61–71.

40. Ibid., 54.

41. David R. Nienhaus, *Not by Paul Alone: The Formation of the Catholic Epistle Collection and the Christian Canon* (Waco, TX: Baylor University Press, 2007) 22.

42. Nienhaus, *Not by Paul Alone*, 229–31.

43. Adamson, *James*, 24.

44. Ibid., 31.

45. Douglas J. Moo, *The Letter of James* (Grand Rapids: Eerdmans / Leicester: Apollos, 2000) 10–11.

46. See Martin Hengel, *Judaism and Hellenism*, 2 vols. (Philadelphia: Fortress, 1974).

47. Moo, *The Letter of James*, 19–20.

48. Johnson, *The Letter of James*, 114.

49. Ibid., 118.

50. Q is short for *Quelle* which means "source" in German. Scholars think that when one compares the similarities and differences among Matthew, Mark and Luke (the Synoptic Gospels), there must be some kind of literary dependence between the three gospels. The task of determining what this dependence may be is called the Synoptic Problem. The most commonly held solution to the problem is that the Gospel of Mark was used by Matthew and Luke. In addition, Matthew and Luke drew upon a common body of materials, primarily teachings and parables of Jesus that are not contained in the Gospel of Mark. This "source" was named *Quelle*, but a written version of it has not been found. Its genre;

that of a sayings source, is comparable to other documents, such as the *Gospel of Thomas*, which consists solely of sayings and teachings of Jesus.

51. Johnson, *The Letter of James*, 121.

52. Richard Bauckham, "James and Jesus," in *The Brother of Jesus*, 104.

53. Ibid., 106.

54. Davids, *The Epistle of James*, 13.

55. Hartin, *James of Jerusalem*, 93.

56. Vouga, *L'Épître de Saint Jacques*, 37.

57. Dibelius, *James*, 66.

58. Matthias Konradt, *Christliche Existenz nach dem Jakobusbrief: Eine Studie zu seiner soteriologischen und ethischen Konzeption* (Göttingen: Vandenhoeck & Ruprecht, 1998) 64.

59. Hutchinson Edgar, *Has God Not Chosen the Poor?* 100–101.

60. Matt Jackson-McCabe, "A Letter to the Twelve Tribes in the Diaspora: Wisdom and 'Apocalyptic' Eschatology in the Letter of James," *SBLSP* 35 (1996) 515.

61. Penner, *The Epistle of James and Eschatology*, 182–83.

62. Cargal, *Restoring the Diaspora*, 45–49.

63. Hartin, *James*, 52.

64. Hartin, *James of Jerusalem*, 95.

65. Ibid.

66. Hartin, *James*, 55

67. Ibid.

68. Dale C. Allison Jr., "The Fiction of James and its *Sitz im Leben*," *RB* 118 (2001) 529–70.

69. Ibid., 570.

70. Ibid.

71. John S. Kloppenborg, "Diaspora Discourse: The Construction of *Ethos* in James," *NTS* 53 (2007) 242–70.

72. Ibid., 254–55.

73. Ibid., 270.

Chapter Three: Thematic Issues in James

1. Martin Luther, *Word and Sacrament I*, Luther's Works 35, E. T. Bachman, ed. (Philadelphia: Muhlenberg Press, 1960) 395–97.

2. It is important to grant, however, that in his *Preface to the New Testament*, Luther said that there were some good teachings in James.

3. See Johnson, *James*, 114.

4. William F. Brosend II, *James and Jude* (Cambridge: Cambridge University Press, 2004) 3–5.

5. Margaret M. Mitchell, "The Letter of James as a Document of Paulinism?" in *Reading James with New Eyes*, 75–98.

6. Vasiliki Limberis, "The Provenance of the Caliphate Church: James 2:17–26 and Galatians 3 Reconsidered," in *Early Christian Interpretation of the Scriptures of Israel: Investigations and Proposals*, Craig A. Evans and James A. Sanders, eds. (Sheffield: Sheffield Academic Press, 1997) 402.

7. Ibid., 409.

8. R. Jason Coker, "Nativism in James 2:14–26: A Post-Colonial Reading?" in *Reading James with New Eyes*, 27.

9. Ibid., 39–40.

10. Ibid., 47.

11. Ibid., 48.

12. Popkes, *Der Brief*, 43.

13. Tsuji, *Glaube zwischen Vollkommenheit und Verweltlichung*, 16.

14. Kari Syreeni, "James and the Pauline Legacy: Power Play in Corinth?" in *Fair Play: Diversity and Conflicts in Early Christianity. Essays in Honour of Heikki Räisänen*, Ismo Dunderberg, Christopher Tuckett and Kari Syreeni, eds. (Leiden: Brill, 2002) 434.

15. For Johnson's discussion of James and Paul, see his *The Letter of James*, 58–64.

16. Ibid., 64.

17. Hartin's discussion of faith and works in James and Paul is found in his *James*, 163–71.

18. Donald J. Verseput, "Reworking the Puzzle of Faith and Deeds in James 2:14–26," *NTS* 43 (1997) 104–5.

19. Ibid., 115.

20. Penner, *Epistle of James and Eschatology*, 72–73.

21. Ibid., 68.

22. See Robert W. Wall, "A Unifying Theology of the Catholic Epistles. A Canonical Approach," in *The Catholic Epistles and the Tradition*, 43–71.

23. Nienhuis, *Not by Paul Alone*, 22.

24. Ibid., 236.

25. Margaret M. Mitchell, "The Letter of James as a Document of Paulinism?" in *Reading James with New Eyes*, 79.

26. Ibid., 80.

27. For example, Martin Dibelius's influential commentary, discussed in an earlier chapter, states that the Letter of James *"has no 'theology'"* (emphasis his) (*James*, 21).

28. Konradt, *Christliche Existenz*, 310.

29. See Klein, *"Ein vollkommenes Werk,"* 43–81.

30. Patrick J. Hartin, *A Spirituality of Perfection. Faith in Action in the Letter of James* (Collegeville, MN: Liturgical Press, 1999) 26.

31. See ibid., 57–92.

32. Ibid., 53.

33. Wesley Hiram Wachob, "The Apocalyptic Intertexture of the Epistle of James," in *The Intertexture of Apocalyptic Discourse in the New Testament*, Duane F. Watson, ed. (Atlanta: SBL, 2002) 183.

34. Ibid., 185.

35. See Penner, *The Epistle of James*, 121–213.

36. Ibid., 212.

37. See, for example, Ulrick Luck, "Der Jakobusbrief und die Theologie des Paulus," *ThGl* 61 (1971) 161–79.

38. Peter H. Davids, "The Epistle of James in Modern Discussion," *ANRW* 2.25.5 (1988) 3644.

39. Ibid., 3645.

40. Andrew Chester and Ralph P. Martin, *The Theology of the Letters of James, Peter and Jude* (Cambridge: Cambridge University Press, 1994) 39.

41. Jackson-McCabe, "A Letter to the Twelve Tribes in the Diaspora," 516.

42. Patrick J. Hartin, " 'Who is Wise and Understanding Among You?' (James 3:13). An Analysis of Wisdom, Eschatology and Apocalypticism in the Epistle of James," *SBLSP* 35 (1996) 500.

43. Ibid., 495–96.

44. Matt Jackson-McCabe, "The Messiah Jesus in the Mythic World of James," *JBL* 122 (2003) 727.

45. Ibid., 730.

46. Chester and Martin, *The Theology*, 43.

47. Ibid., 37.

48. Luke Timothy Johnson, *Brother of Jesus, Friend of God* (Grand Rapids: Eerdmans, 2004) 126.

49. See ibid., 132.

50. See ibid., 134.

51. Matt Jackson-McCabe, *Logos and Law in the Letter of James. The Law of Nature, the Law of Moses and the Law of Freedom* (Leiden: Brill, 2001) 27.

52. See Elliott, "The Epistle of James," 73.

53. Ibid., 79.

54. Darian Lockett, " 'Unstained by the World': Purity and Pollution as an Indicator of Cultural Interaction in the Letter of James," in *Reading James with New Eyes*, 51. See also, Darian Lockett, *Purity and Worldview in the Epistle of James* (London: T & T Clark, 2008).

55. Ibid., 74.

56. Joel Marcus, "The Evil Inclination in the Epistle of James," *CBQ* 44 (1982) 620–21. Johnson (*James*, 194) disagrees with Marcus, stating that James shows "no real trace here of a psychology of the 'two inclinations.' "

57. Marcus, "The Evil Inclination," 620.

58. Ibid., 621.

59. Walter T. Wilson, "Sin as Sex and Sex with Sin: The Anthropology of James 1:12–15," *HTR* 95 (2002) 161–63.

60. J. L. P. Wolmarens, "Male and Female Sexual Imagery: James 1:14–15, 18," *Acta Patristica et Byzantina* 5 (1994) 134–41.

61. Wilson, "Sin as Sex," 164.

62. Ibid., 168.

63. One of my former students, who had become exceedingly wealthy through business ventures, once commented to me that she found the Letter of James quite offensive.

64. For example, liberation theologian Elsa Tamez writes that "[i]t is good that many poor people rejoice to find in James a friend who brings them good news, while others suffer a crisis of Christian identity, because James says that to be a Christian requires the fulfillment of certain conditions. The identity crisis that James causes for us is also a reason for joy" (*The Scandalous Message of James. Faith Without Works Is Dead* [New York: Crossroad, 1990] 79).

65. John Calvin, *Commentaries on the Catholic Epistles*, trans. John Owen (Grand Rapids: Eerdmans, 1948) 300.

66. As Peter H. Davids ("The Test of Wealth," in *The Missions of James, Peter and Paul*, 379) states, "the one thing that we can be sure of is that James consistently describes the wealthier people within the Christian community negatively, while 'the rich' (outside the community) are roundly condemned."

67. Pedrito U. Maynard-Reid, *Poverty and Wealth in James* (Maryknoll, NY: Orbis, 1987).

68. Ibid., 97.

69. Ibid.

70. Patrick A. Tiller, "The Rich and Poor in James. An Apocalyptic Proclamation," *SBLSP* 37 (1998) 919.

71. Alicia Batten, "Ideological Strategies in James," in *Reading James with New Eyes*, 76.

72. John S. Kloppenborg, "Response to 'Riches, the Rich and God's Judgment in 1 Enoch 92—105 and the Gospel According to Luke' and 'Revisiting the Rich and the Poor in 1 Enoch 92—105 and the Gospel According to Luke,'" in *George W. E. Nickelsburg in Perspective: An Ongoing Dialogue of Learning*, Jacob Neusner and Alan J. Avery-Peck, eds. (Leiden: E. J. Brill, 2003) 583.

73. Ibid., 585.

74. See Richard Saller, *Personal Patronage under the Early Empire* (Cambridge: Cambridge University Press, 1982) 7.

75. See Peter Garnsey, *Famine and Food Supply in the Graeco-Roman World. Responses to Risk and Crisis* (Cambridge: Cambridge University Press, 1988) 58.

76. Nancy Vhymeister, "The Rich Man in James 2: Does Ancient Patronage Illumine the Text?" *AUSS* 33 (1995) 283.

77. John S. Kloppenborg, "Patronage Avoidance in James," *HTS* 55 (1999) 765. Kloppenborg refers to some comparable ancient Greek satirical writings such as Lucian's *Nigrinus* 21 as well as Lucian's *Gallus* 12.

78. John S. Kloppenborg, "Status und Wohltägtigkeit bei Paulus und Jakobus," in *Von Jesus zum Christus. Christologischen Studien. Festgabe für Paul Hoffmann zum 65. Geburtstag*, R. Hoppe and U. Busse, eds. (Berlin: Walter de Gruyter, 1998) 127–54.

79. Ibid., 154.

80. Ibid.

81. Hutchinson Edgar, *Has God Not Chosen the Poor?* 122.

82. Alicia Batten, "God in the Letter of James: Patron or Benefactor?" *NTS* 50 (2004) 267.

83. Luke Timothy Johnson, *Brother of Jesus, Friend of God*, 164–65.

84. Ibid., 165–66.

85. Ibid., 167.

86. William R. Baker, *Personal Speech-Ethics in the Epistle of James* (Tübingen: Mohr, 1995) 283.

87. Ibid., 284–85.

88. Ibid., 287.

Chapter Four: James and the Sayings of Jesus

1. In addition, since the late nineteenth century some scholars have argued that the reference to Jesus Christ in Jas 1:1 is a later interpolation. See L. Massebieau, "L'épître de Jacques est-elle l'oeuvre d'un chrétien?" *RHR* 32 (1895) 249–85; and F. Spitta, "Der Brief des Jakobus," *Zur Geschichte und Literatur des Urchristentums*, vol. 2 (Göttingen: Vandenhoeck & Ruprecht, 1896) 158–77.

2. Jas 2:8 (Lev 19:18); 2:11a (Exod 20:13; Deut 5:17); 2:11b (Exod 20:15; Deut 5:17); 2:23 (Gen 15:6); 4:5 (which does not directly quote, but appears to be an allusion to Gen 6:3); 4:6 (Prov 3:34).

3. Dean B. Deppe, *The Sayings of Jesus in the Epistle of James* (doctoral dissertation, Free University of Amsterdam, 1989) 7–30.

4. Ibid., 231–33.

5. This point is made by Kloppenborg, "The Reception of Jesus Traditions," 94.

6. Deppe, *The Sayings of Jesus*, 220–21.

7. Ibid., 223.

8. Ibid., 222–23. Deppe provides a full listing of the synoptic parallels.

9. Ibid., 221.

10. Ibid., 222.

11. Ibid., 218.

12. Ibid., 223.

13. Luke Timothy Johnson with Wesley H. Wachob, "The Sayings of Jesus in the Letter of James," in Johnson, *Brother of Jesus, Friend of God*, 153.

14. Ibid., 154.

15. Patrick J. Hartin, *James and the Q Sayings of Jesus*, 140–42.

16. Ibid., 152–54.

17. Ibid., 243.

18. Bauckham, *James*, 86.

19. Ibid., 76.

20. Ibid.

21. Ibid., 79.

22. Ibid., 83–84.

23. Ibid., 87.

24. Ibid., 87–88.

25. Ibid., 108.

26. Wachob, *The Voice of Jesus*, 199.

27. Ibid., 137.

28. Ibid., 139.

29. Ibid., 150–51.

30. Kloppenborg, "The Reception of Jesus Traditions," 121.

31. Ibid., 138.

32. Ibid., 139.

33. Ibid.

34. Ibid., 141.

35. John S. Kloppenborg, "The Emulation of the Jesus Tradition in the Letter of James," *Reading James with New Eyes*, 121–50.

36. Ibid., 138.

37. Ibid., 139.

38. Ibid., 140.

BIBLIOGRAPHY

Adamson, James B. *James. The Man and His Message*. Grand Rapids: Eerdmans, 1989.

Allison, Dale C. "The Fiction of James and its *Sitz im Leben*." *RB* 118 (2001): 529–70.

Aune, David E. *The New Testament in Its Literary Environment*. LEC 8. Philadelphia: Westminster, 1987.

Baasland, Ernst. "Literarische Form, Thematik und geschichtliche Einordung des Jakobusbriefes." *ANRW* 2.25.5 (1988): 3646–84.

———. *Jakobsbrevet*. KNT 16. Uppsala: EFS, 1992.

Baker, William R. *Personal Speech-Ethics in the Epistle of James*. Tübingen: Mohr, 1995.

Batten, Alicia. *Unworldly Friendship: 'The Epistle of Straw' Reconsidered*. Unpublished doctoral dissertation. University of St. Michael's College, 2000.

———. "God in the Letter of James: Patron or Benefactor?" *NTS* 50 (2004): 257–72.

———. "Ideological Strategies in James." In *Reading James with New Eyes. Methodological Reassessments of the Letter of James*, edited by Robert L. Webb and John S. Kloppenborg, 6–26. LNTS 342. London: T & T Clark, 2007.

Bauckham, Richard. *James. Wisdom of James, Disciple of Jesus the Sage*. New Testament Readings. London: Routledge, 1999.

Berger, Klaus. *Formgeschichte des Neuen Testament*. Heidelberg: Quelle & Meyer, 1984.

Bernheim, Pierre Antoine. *James, Brother of Jesus.* Translated by John Bowden. London: SCM Press, 1997.

Bitzer, Lloyd. "The Rhetorical Situation." *Philosophy and Rhetoric* 1 (1968): 1–14.

Brosend II, William F. *James and Jude.* NCBC. Cambridge: Cambridge University Press, 2004.

Cargal, Timothy. *Restoring the Diaspora: Discursive Structure and Purpose in the Epistle of James.* SBLDS 144. Atlanta: Scholars Press, 1993.

Chester, Andrew, and Ralph P. Martin. *The Theology of the Letters of James, Peter and Jude.* New Testament Theology. Cambridge: Cambridge University Press, 1994.

Chilton, Bruce, and Craig A. Evans, eds. *James the Just and Christian Origins.* NovTSup 98. Leiden: E. J. Brill, 1999.

Chilton, Bruce, and Jacob Neusner, eds., *The Brother of Jesus. James the Just and His Mission.* Louisville: Westminster/John Knox Press, 2001.

Coker, R. Jason. "Nativism in James 2:14–26: A Post-Colonial Reading?" In *Reading James with New Eyes. Methodological Reassessments of the Letter of James,* edited by Robert L. Webb and John S. Kloppenborg, 27–48. LNTS 342. London: T & T Clark, 2007.

Crotty, Robert B. "The Literary Structure of the Letter of James." *ABR* 40 (1992): 45–57.

Davids, Peter H. *The Epistle of James: A Commentary on the Greek Text.* NIGTC. Grand Rapids: Eerdmans, 1982.

———. "The Epistle of James in Modern Discussion." *ANRW* 2.25.2 (1988): 3621–45.

———. "Palestinian Traditions in the Epistle of James." In *James the Just and Christian Origins,* edited by Bruce Chilton and Craig A. Evans, 33–57. NovTSup 98. Leiden: Brill, 1999.

———. "The Test of Wealth." In *The Missions of James, Peter and Paul. Tensions in Early Christianity,* edited by Bruce Chilton and Craig Evans, 355–84. NovTSup 115. Leiden: Brill, 2005.

Deppe, Dean B. *The Sayings of Jesus in the Epistle of James.* Doctoral dissertation. Free University of Amsterdam, 1989.

Dibelius, Martin. *James. A Commentary on the Epistle of James.* Revised by Heinrich Greeven. Translated by Michael A. Williams. Hermeneia. Philadelphia: Fortress, 1976.

Edgar, David Hutchinson. *Has God Not Chosen the Poor? The Social Setting of the Epistle of James.* JSNTSup 206. Sheffield: Sheffield Academic Press, 2001.

Elliott, John H. "The Epistle of James in Rhetorical Social Scientific Perspective. Holiness-Wholeness and Patterns of Replication." *BTB* 23 (1993): 71–81.

Francis, Fred O. "The Form and Function of the Opening and Closing Paragraphs of James and 1 John." *ZNW* 61 (1970): 110–26.

Frankenmölle, Hubert. "Das semantische Netz des Jakobusbriefes. Zur Einheit eines umstritten Briefes." *BZ* 34 (1990): 161–97.

———. *Der Brief des Jakobus.* ÖTK 17/1–2. Gütersloh: Gütersloher Verlaghaus, 1994.

Gammie, John J. "Paraenetic Literature: Toward the Morphology of a Secondary Genre." *Semeia* 50 (1990): 41–77.

Garnsey, Peter. *Famine and Food Supply in the Graeco-Roman World. Responses to Risk and Crisis.* Cambridge: Cambridge University Press, 1988.

Harner, Philip B. *What Are They Saying About the Catholic Epistles?* New York/Mahwah, NJ: Paulist, 2004.

Hartin, Patrick J. *James and the Q Sayings of Jesus.* JSNTSup 47. Sheffield: JSOT Press, 1991.

———. " 'Who is Wise and Understanding Among You' (James 3:13)? An Analysis of Wisdom, Eschatology and Apocalypticism in the Epistle of James." *SBLSP* 35 (1996): 483–503.

———. *A Spirituality of Perfection. Faith in Action in the Letter of James.* Collegeville: Liturgical Press, 1999.

———. *James.* Sacra Pagina Series 13. Collegeville: Liturgical Press, 2003.

———. *James of Jerusalem. Heir to Jesus of Nazareth.* Interfaces. Collegeville, MN: Michael Glazier, 2004.

Hengel, Martin. *Judaism and Hellenism.* 2 vols. Philadelphia: Fortress, 1974.

Hughes, F. W. *Early Christian Rhetoric and 2 Thessalonians.* JSNTSup 30. Sheffield: Sheffield Academic Press, 1989.

Jackson-McCabe, Matt. "A Letter to the Twelve Tribes in the Diaspora: Wisdom and 'Apocalyptic' Eschatology in the Letter of James." *SBLSP* 35 (1996): 504–17.

————. *Logos and Law in the Letter of James. The Law of Nature, the Law of Moses and the Law of Freedom*. NovTSup 100. Leiden: Brill, 2001.

————. "The Messiah Jesus in the Mythic World of James." *JBL* 122 (2003): 701–30.

Jackson-McCabe, Matt., ed. *Jewish Christianity Reconsidered. Rethinking Ancient Groups and Texts*. Minneapolis: Fortress, 2007.

Johnson, Luke Timothy. "Taciturnity and True Religion: James 1:26–27." In *Greeks, Romans and Christians. Essays in Honor of Abraham J. Malherbe*, edited by David L. Balch, Everett Ferguson and Wayne A. Meeks, 329–39. Minneapolis: Fortress, 1990.

————. *The Letter of James*. AB 37A. New York: Doubleday, 1995.

————. *Brother of Jesus, Friend of God*. Grand Rapids, Cambridge: Eerdmans, 2004.

Kennedy, George A. *A New History of Classical Rhetoric*. Princeton: Princeton University Press, 1994.

Klein, Martin. *"Ein vollkommenes Werk": Vollkommenheit, Gesetz und Gericht als theologische Themen des Jakobusbriefes*. BWANT 139. Stuttgart: Kohlhammer, 1995.

Kloppenborg, John S. "Status und Wohltägtigkeit bei Paulus und Jakobus." In *Von Jesus zum Christus. Christologischen Studien. Festgabe für Paul Hoffman zum 65. Geburtstag*, edited by R. Hoppe and U. Busse, 127–54. BZNW 93. Berlin: Walter de Gruyter, 1998.

————. "Patronage Avoidance in James." *HTS* 55 (1999): 755–94.

————. "Response to 'Riches, the Rich and God's Judgment in 1 Enoch 92—105 and the Gospel According to Luke' and 'Revisiting the Rich and the Poor in 1 Enoch 92—105 and the Gospel According to Luke.'" In *George W. E. Nickelsburg in Perspective: An Ongoing Dialogue of Learning*, edited by Jacob Neusner and Alan J. Avery-Peck, 572–85. Leiden: Brill, 2003.

————. "The Reception of Jesus Traditions in James." In *The Catholic Epistles and the Tradition*, edited by J. Schlosser, 93–141. BETL 176. Leuven: Peeters, 2004.

————. "Diaspora Discourse: The Construction of *Ethos* in James." *NTS* 53 (2007): 242–70.

————. "The Emulation of the Jesus Tradition in the Letter of James." In *Reading James with New Eyes. Methodological Reassessments of the*

Letter of James, edited by Robert L. Webb and John S. Kloppenborg, 121–50. LNTS 342. London: T & T Clark, 2007.

Konradt, Matthias. *Christliche Existenz nach dem Jakobusbrief: Eine Studie zu seiner soteriologischen und ethischen Konzeption*. SUNT 22. Göttingen: Vandehoeck & Ruprecht, 1998.

Laws, Sophie. *The Epistle of James*. BNTC. London: Adam and Charles Black, 1980.

Limberis, Vasiliki. "The Provenance of the Caliphate Church: James 2:17–26 and Galatians 3 Reconsidered." In *Early Christian Interpretation of the Scriptures of Israel: Investigations and Proposals*, edited by Craig A. Evans and James A. Sanders, 397–420. JSNTSup 148. Sheffield: Sheffield Academic Press, 1997.

Llewellyn, S. R. "The Prescript of James." *NovT* 39 (1997): 385–93.

Lockett, Darian. "'Unstained by the World': Purity and Pollution as an Indicator of Cultural Interaction in the Letter of James." In *Reading James with New Eyes. Methodological Reassessments of the Letter of James*, edited by Robert L. Webb and John S. Kloppenborg, 49–74. LNTS 342. London: T & T Clark, 2007.

———. *Purity and Worldview in the Epistle of James*. LNTS 366. London: T & T Clark, 2008.

Luck, Ulrick. "Der Jakosbusbrief und die Theologie des Paulus." *ThGl* 61 (1971): 161–79.

Mack, Burton L. *Rhetoric and the New Testament*. GBS. Minneapolis: Fortress, 1990.

Marcus, Joel. "The Evil Inclination in the Epistle of James." *CBQ* 44 (1982): 606–21.

Martin, Ralph P. *James*. WBC 48. Waco: Word Books, 1988.

Massebieau, L. "L'épître de Jacques est-elle l'oeuvre d'un chrétien?" *RHR* 32 (1895): 249–85.

Maynard-Reid, Pedrito U. *Poverty and Wealth in James*. Maryknoll: Orbis, 1987. Reprint Eugene, OR: Wipf and Stock, 2004.

Mitchell, Margaret M. "The Letter of James as a Document of Paulinism?" In *Reading James with New Eyes. Methodological Reassessments of the Letter of James*, edited by John S. Kloppenborg and Robert L. Webb, 75–98. LNTS 342. London: T & T Clark, 2007.

Moo, Douglas. *The Letter of James*. Pillar New Testament Commentary. Leicester: Apollos; Grand Rapids: Eerdmans, 2000.

Myllykoski, Matti. "James the Just in History and Tradition: Perspectives of Past and Present Scholarship (Part I)." *CBR* 5.1 (2006) 73–122.

Niebuhr, Karl-Wilhem. "Der Jakobusbrief im Licht frühjüdischer Diasporabriefe." *NTS* 44 (1998): 420–43.

Nienhaus, David R. *Not by Paul Alone: The Formation of the Catholic Epistle Collection and the Christian Canon.* Waco, TX: Baylor University Press, 2007.

Painter, John. *Just James: The Brother of Jesus in History and Tradition.* Columbia: University of South Carolina Press, 1997.

———. "The Power of Words: Rhetoric in James and Paul." In *The Missions of James, Peter and Paul. Tensions in Early Christianity*, edited by Bruce Chilton and Craig Evans, 253–73. NovTSup 115. Leiden: Brill, 2005.

Pardee, Dennis. *Handbook of Ancient Hebrew Letters.* SBLSBS 15. Chico, CA: Scholars Press, 1982.

Penner, Todd C. "The Epistle of James in Current Research." *CR:BS* 7 (1999): 257–308.

Perdue, Leo G. "Paraenesis and the Epistle of James." *ZNW* 72 (1981): 241–56.

———. "The Death of the Sage and Moral Exhortation: From Ancient Near Eastern Instructions to Graeco-Roman Paraenesis." *Semeia* 50 (1990): 81–109.

Popkes, Wiard. "James and Paraenesis Reconsidered." In *Texts and Contexts. Biblical Texts in Their Textual and Situational Contexts*, edited by Tord Fornberg and David Hellholm, 535–61. Oslo: Scandinavian University Press, 1995.

———. *Der Brief des Jakobus.* THKNT 14. Leipzig: Evangelische Verlagsanstalt, 2001.

Penner, Todd C. *The Epistle of James and Eschatology. Re-reading an Ancient Christian Letter.* JSNTSup 121. Sheffield: Sheffield Academic Press, 1996.

Reese, James M. "The Exegete as Sage: Hearing the Message of James." *BTB* 12 (1982): 82–85.

Robbins, Vernon K. "Writing as a Rhetorical Act in Plutarch and the Gospels." In *Persuasive Artistry: Studies in New Testament Rhetoric in Honor of George A. Kennedy*, 157–86. Sheffield: JSOT Press, 1991.

Ropes, James Hardy. *A Critical and Exegetical Commentary on the Epistle of St. James*. ICC. Edinburgh: T & T Clark, 1916.

Saller, Richard. *Personal Patronage under the Early Empire*. Cambridge: Cambridge University Press, 1982.

Schlosser, J., ed., *The Catholic Epistles and the Tradition*. BETL 176. Leuven: Peeters, 2004.

Spitta, F. "Der Brief des Jakobus." In *Zur Geschichte und Literatur des Urchristentums*. Volume 2, 158–77. Göttingen: Vandenhoeck & Ruprecht, 1896.

Stowers, Stanley. "The Diatribe." In *Greco-Roman Literature and the New Testament*, edited by David E. Aune, 71–83. SBLSBS 21. Atlanta: Scholars Press, 1988.

Syreeni, Kari. "James and the Pauline Legacy: Power Play in Corinth?" In *Fair Play: Diversity and Conflicts in Early Christianity. Essays in Honour of Heikki Räisänen*, edited by Ismo Dunderberg, Christopher Tuckett and Kari Syreeni, 397–437. NovTSup 103. Leiden: Brill, 2002.

Tamez, Elsa. *The Scandalous Message of James. Faith without Works Is Dead*. New York: Crossroad, 1992.

Taylor, Mark E. "Recent Scholarship on the Structure of James." *Currents in Biblical Research* 3.1 (2004): 86–115.

———. *A Text-Linguistic Investigation into the Discourse Structure of James*. LNTS 311. London: T & T Clark, 2006.

Thurén, Lauri. "Risky Rhetoric in James?" *NovT* 37 (1995): 262–84.

Tiller, Patrick A. "The Rich and Poor in James. An Apocalyptic Proclamation." *SBLSP* 37 (1998): 909–20.

Tollefson, Kenneth D. "The Epistle of James as Dialectical Discourse." *BTB* 21 (1997): 62–69.

Tsuji, Manabu. *Glaube zwischen Vollkommenheit und Verweltlichung: Eine Untersuchung zur literarischen Gestalt und zur inhaltlichen Kohärenz des Jakobusbriefes*. WUNT 2/93. Tübingen: J.C.B. Mohr (Siebeck), 1997.

van der Westhuizen, J. D. N. "Stylistic Techniques and their Functions in James 2:14–26." *Neot* 25 (1991): 89–107.

Verseput, Donald J. "Reworking the Puzzle of Faith and Deeds in James 2:14–26." *NTS* 43 (1997): 97–115.

Vhymeister, Nancy. "The Rich Man in James 2: Does Ancient Patronage Illumine the Text?" *AUSS* 33 (1995): 265–83.

Vouga, François. *L'Épître de Saint Jacques*. CNT 13A. Geneva: Labor et Fides, 1984.

Wachob, Wesley Hiram. *The Voice of Jesus in the Social Rhetoric of James*. SNTS Monograph Series 106. Cambridge: Cambridge University Press, 2000.

————. "The Apocalyptic Intertexture of the Epistle of James." In *The Intertexture of Apocalyptic Discourse in the New Testament*, edited by Duane F. Watson, 165–85. SBLSymS 14. Atlanta: SBL, 2002.

————. "The Languages of 'Household' and 'Kingdom' in the Letter of James: A Socio-Rhetorical Study." In *Reading James with New Eyes. Methodological Reassessments of the Letter of James*, edited by Robert L. Webb and John S. Kloppenborg, 151–68. LNTS 342. London: T & T Clark, 2007.

Wall, Robert M. *Community of the Wise. The Letter of James*. New Testament in Context. Valley Forge, PA: Trinity, 1997.

————. "A Unifying Theology of the Catholic Epistles. A Canonical Approach." In *The Catholic Epistles and the Tradition*, edited by J. Schlosser, 43–71. BETL 176. Leuven: Peeters, 2004.

Watson, Duane F. "James 2 in Light of Greco-Roman Schemes of Argumentation." *NTS* 39 (1993): 94–129.

————. "The Rhetoric of James 3:1–12 and a Classical Pattern of Argumentation." *NovT* 35 (1993): 48–64.

————. "A Reassessment of the Rhetoric of the Epistle of James and Its Implications for Christian Origins." In *Reading James with New Eyes. Methodological Reassessments of the Letter of James*, edited by Robert L. Webb and John S. Kloppenborg, 99–120. LNTS 342. London: T & T Clark, 2007.

Watson, Duane F., and Alan J. Hauser. *Rhetorical Criticism of the Bible. A Comprehensive Bibliography with Notes on History and Method*. Leiden: Brill, 1994.

Webb, Robert L., and John S. Kloppenborg, eds., *Reading James with New Eyes. Methodological Reassessments of the Letter of James*. LNTS 342. London: T & T Clark, 2007.

Wilson, Walter T. "Sin as Sex and Sex with Sin: The Anthropology of James 1:12–15." *HTR* 95 (2002): 147–68.

Wolmarens, J. L. P. "Male and Female Sexual Imagery: James 1:14–15, 18." *Acta Patristica et Byzantina* 5 (1994): 134–41.

Wuellner, Wilhelm. "Der Jakobusbrief im Licht der Rhetorik und Textpragmatik." *LB* 43 (1978): 5–66.

Yates, Jonathan P. "The Reception of the Epistle of James in the Latin West: Did Athanasius Play a Role?" In *The Catholic Epistles and the Tradition*, edited by J. Schlosser, 273–88. BETL 176. Leuven: Peeters, 2004.

Other Books in the Series